THE GAY AFFAIR

Praise for Dr. Carol Swain and *The Gay Affair*

"Carol Swain's new book dissects the failure of DEI and plagiarism through the story of former Harvard president Claudine Gay. Swain makes the case that justice will not be served until universities abandon racialist policies and make academic integrity the standard for all."
— **Christopher Rufo,** journalist, writer, filmmaker, activist

"Dr. Carol Swain understands all too well how higher education has been hijacked by the left but without common sense accountability. Her latest book about the scandal surrounding the first black Harvard president—*The Gay Affair: Harvard, Plagiarism, and the Death of Academic Integrity*—is an insightful and inside look at Harvard's humiliating failure to conduct due diligence on selecting a leader and why it matters regardless of race."
— **Gov. Mike Huckabee,** appointed US Ambassador to Israel

"Striving for excellence was once a high priority for Black Americans. Slavery, Jim Crow racism, and discrimination were barriers that spurred many Blacks to defy racism by working harder and smarter. *The Gay Affair* illustrates the differences between Carol Swain and Claudine Gay, who represent different generations, socioeconomic backgrounds, and value systems. Unfortunately, the victimization culture of today has been a setback for many young black Americans who have had every opportunity to shine."
— **Robert L. Woodson,** founder and president of the Woodson Center, 1776 Unites, and Voices of Black Mothers United.

"Organizations that sacrifice merit in pursuit of extraneous "diversity" considerations, such as skin color and sexual preference, will tend to decline in quality. *The Gay Affair* exposes this dynamic at Harvard University—an institution formerly synonymous with excellence. Claudine Gay's leadership failures during the campus antisemitism crisis amid subsequent plagiarism revelations exposed the folly of prioritizing diversity over competence. Carol Swain depicts the shallow and destructive character of the DEI regime."
— **Christopher Schorr,** senior policy analyst, America First Policy Institute

"It is undeniable that there's a systemic crisis throughout academia reaching into every facet of academic life: from teaching and curriculum to administration and even research. In this timely and revealing book by Carol Swain, the curtain gets pulled back on some of the most prominent and ugly problems poisoning higher education in America and around the world."
— **James Lindsay,** founder of New Discourses

"Carol Swain has written a timely and incisive critique of the challenges facing higher education. With her characteristic rigor and sharp insights, Swain unpacks the cultural and institutional factors undermining accountability and intellectual honesty at one of the world's leading universities. This book is an essential read for anyone concerned about academic integrity's future."
— **Dr. Robert J. Pacienza,** senior pastor of Coral Ridge Presbyterian Church, Fort Lauderdale, Florida

"Doctor Swain's latest book is a clear and convincing indictment, not only of Claudine Gay but also of Harvard's leadership which selected her as president, despite her unimpressive resume and rumors of plagiarism, which have been found to be true."
— **Robert J. Shillman**, PhD, founder, Cognex Corporation

"In *The Gay Affair*, Dr. Swain takes us on a tour de force that defines the inevitable hardships a legitimate scholar faces confronting the hypocrisy of the DEI agenda that confers a privileged status to minority candidates espousing neo-Marxist ideology. Dr. Swain sets the record straight regarding her award-winning work that Claudine Gay stole from to promote herself."
— **Jerome R. Corsi, PhD,** Harvard graduate and *New York Times* bestselling author and political commentator

"Harvard and similar institutions once comprising the elite vanguard of Western civilization have inanely cast off the lofty and laudable principles that created them. Quite tellingly, honor and integrity are the most recent to be abandoned, and Carol Swain—in a particular position to know the gory details—tells us the grim story, which is a vitally important one for our time. Only by understanding what happened can we, by God's grace, ever find our way back."
— **Eric Metaxas,** host of *Socrates in the City*, and author of *Bonhoeffer: Pastor, Martyr, Prophet, Spy*

"Carol Swain's latest book is a vital investigation that holds powerful forces accountable for their abuse of academic integrity through toxic ideology that prioritizes identity over merit. Claudine Gay's failures are a microcosm of widespread rot infecting America's institutions of higher learning, though Carol provides valuable insights on reform that university administrators would be wise to implement."
— **Carrie Sheffield,** Harvard graduate and author of *Motorhome Prophecies: A Journey of Healing and Forgiveness*

THE GAY AFFAIR

Harvard, Plagiarism, and the Death of Academic Integrity

Carol M. Swain, PhD

Foreword by Chanel Rion

Copyright©2025 by Carol M. Swain
All rights reserved. Written permission must be secured from the publisher or the author to use or reproduce any part of this book, except for brief quotations in critical reviews or articles.

ISBNs:
Print edition: 978-1-7374198-4-6
eBook: 978-1-7374198-5-3
Audio book: 978-1-7374198-6-0

Cover design by LACreative.
Cover photo of Harvard University provided by Jorge Salcedo and licensed through
shutterstock.com.
Page design by Win-Win Words LLC.

For Doris Kearns Goodwin, Stephen E. Ambrose, Kevin Kruse, and Claudine Gay for helping to expose the deadly plague of 'plagiaritis' that is killing academic integrity in higher education.

Contents

	Foreword	xi
	Acknowledgments	xvii
	Preface	xix
1	The Gay Resignation	1
2	A 'Plagiaritis' Pandemic?	9
3	Black Sunday	17
4	Hamas Fallout Reaches Harvard	23
5	Plagiarism Déjà Vu	29
6	A Legal Remedy	37
7	Outliers	45
8	Farewell to Oversight	49
	Notes	55
	Appendices:	
	A *Gay and Swain Side-by-Side Comparison*	62
	B *Swain-Harvard Legal Correspondence*	64
	C *My Legal Complaint*	82
	D *Claudine Gay's Dissertation Abstract & Intro*	98
	Author Bio	101

Foreword

THIS IS NO SMALL STORY. The former president of Harvard University stole the work of Dr. Carol Swain and many others. And Dr. Swain is right when she says, "What happens at Harvard affects the entire world." No one has more standing and stature to author this book than Dr. Swain—from whose work and intellectual prowess Harvard's Gay stole.

Harvard University's thirtieth president, Claudine Gay, will go down as nothing more than an alleyway pick-pocket, a petty thief of words and ideas—shockingly brazen, yet too egomaniacal—and DEI protected—to admit her own mediocrity. And that's what plagiarists usually are—exhibits in mediocrity. And that's what the shame of plagiarism is, the shame of mediocrity—but the shame doesn't end there.

Harvard defended Gay to the end using such euphemistic phrases and word-stickers for unquestionable plagiarism as "insufficiently cited" and "duplicative language." After calls for her firing grew deafening, more than five hundred members of the Harvard Faculty had the gall to sign a letter "standing" with Gay against the embarrassing fact that as president of the world's most prestigious university, Gay's scholastic throne was cluttered with plagiaristic lies—plagiarism being a capital offense at most universities.

These faculty-signed emails slid into my inbox as innocuous "updates" for the Harvard diaspora. I was not alone in my outrage. The hypocrisy was breathtaking.

Especially for those who remember.

Foreword

THE HARVARD CHEATING SCANDAL OF 2012

In 2012, I was in the second year of my undergraduate studies, concentrating in International Relations—relieved by then that my homeschool background proved I could thrive in a formal setting. I was having adventures, making friends, building memories, and stacking grades.

I graduated in 2015, with honors, and can attest—Harvard is a place that can change your life. It can just as easily destroy it. One hundred twenty-five Harvard undergrads would learn this the hard way in the Spring of 2012.

Most of the 125 had consulted the Q Guide—the student-circulated course guide—to learn that Govt 1310: Introduction to Congress was an "easy A." Govt 1310, as taught by an assistant professor, was said to have told students, according to the *New York Times*, that attendance was "optional."

I didn't know it then, but my soon-to-be husband, Courtland, was in that class. He escaped the batch of students flagged for plagiarism—he was a loner and didn't like "study groups." This aversion not only drew me to him but saved him from the guillotine of a disastrous episode in Harvard history.

The rest of his classmates were not so lucky. Students reported they were told to form study groups. There were ambiguities about the take-home exams, and what "collaboration" meant. Students reported they were following instructions from a teaching assistant—students met in the same room, discussed the course with the understanding that since the TA suggested the gatherings, and professor told them they could collaborate—none, surely, were about to knowingly ruin their lives and reputations for all time. Who would walk into a class thinking that? So the course was a disaster waiting to happen. Allegedly, a teaching assistant turned everyone in.

Harvard put nearly half the class on academic leave over mere allegations of potential plagiarism.

By summer's end, Harvard publicly announced it was conducting investigations into the students involved. The penalty for plagiarism was not only to get kicked out of Harvard, but to wear a black mark of plagiarism and cheating one's entire life. It might as well have been a felony conviction for theft.

The accused students were devastated. Forced to withdraw from campus in shame, the dreaded black sword of cheating dangled over their heads for months as the Harvard Administrative Board evaluated each case and rendered verdicts every Tuesday. Some students missed an entire year.

Harvard was using their lives, reputations, and futures, as a "teaching moment" to serve as a warning that Harvard does not tolerate plagiarism or cheating.

I had a friend caught up in all this. That friend was ultimately cleared and allowed to return to school but only after sleepless months wondering if one of the biggest lottery tickets of life was now a deadly liability.

HARVARD'S LOST HONOR

Of all the crimes in academia, plagiarism may be the most unforgivable. Plagiarism is the domain stalked by the uniquely untalented and lazy.

When plagiarists steal to survive, as in "get a grade," that's lazy. When plagiarists steal to get ahead, that's theft plain and simple. And likely testament to a subterranean IQ—absent a moral compass.

Harvard had choices; condemn 125 students for plagiarism, blame the assistant professor for faulty instructions, or revert to euphemisms to defend the indefensible. Harvard University was quick to throw the lives of 125 undergraduates under the bus to defend its own policies and faulty decisions in hiring flawed administrators.

In the military, if 125 Navy SEALS were to have been found to have engaged in wrongdoing, under one command, *all* leadership would be immediately relieved of command. That's the standard for the best of the best. Harvard's arrogant inability to acknowledge or apologize for this egregious behavior will not surprise. Arrogance is the modus operandus of America's elite academic class—they see themselves supreme above all—the last word, the final authority. Those

125 students didn't "cheat"—Harvard cheated them. Adding insult to injury, Claudine Gay, whose plagiarism was obvious, wasn't sent home with a black mark. She's still at Harvard today, collecting nearly one million dollars a year in salary and benefits. Harvard's gift to a plagiarist to prove that Harvard is always right and always has the last word.

THE MYTH OF THE MAYA – A VIGNETTE

Academic fraud propagated by sheer elite arrogance is nothing new in academia.

An example—for the good part of the twentieth century, the entire world believed an academic theory that the Ancient Mayans were peaceful philosopher-priests, that Mayan pyramids were quiet ceremonial centers.

When the bodies of hundreds of small children were found nearby, the bodies were dismissed as disease victims. When hieroglyphics indicated violence, hieroglyphics were dismissed as narratives of violence in other tribes—not the Mayans! The Mayans were peaceful! This false academic narrative was driven by one academic, J. Eric Thompson, and an academic class that licked his boots. Thompson, once credited as genius, is widely dismissed today as one of the most mistaken scholars of all time—an academic who used his status to quash any dissenting evidence challenging the false thesis upon which he built his ego.

Thompson was wrong, period. The Mayans tore out the hearts of living children en masse and conducted bloody wars. Thompson was the single biggest obstacle to the study of the Mayans for nearly a century. This is academic arrogance practiced widely to hinder truth and academic progress.

Harvard claims that not only is it the paragon of academic excellence, but implicitly, the paragon of truth and virtue—its motto, *Veritas*. The Gay story refutes that. This arrogance will not only hinder progress and excellence, but will suffocate all that is good at Harvard and in academia.

Foreword

THE PERSON WITH THE MOST STANDING TO WRITE THIS BOOK

I, like so many, was first introduced to Carol Swain when she was a professor having taught at Princeton, Duke, and Vanderbilt. I saw her speak with such eloquence on the big screen—in Dinesh D'Souza's film, *Hillary's America*. Carol Swain had an edge and a bite grounded in substance, a powerful wit and repartee, a beauty that comes from a person of realized gratitude. I did not know then that just a few years later, I would call this woman a friend, a mentor, and a true inspiration. She inspired me to go to law school, attended my wedding, held my newborn son, and became my confidante. Her wise and brutal honesty, her profound outlook, her serene sense of duty to God and Country all make her a great American. She has become a national treasure for her insight, and her insight speaks for itself through her often-cited publications and writings.

Dr. Swain is so many things the mediocre could only hope to emulate. Her story of perseverance against the tide of the impossible is real, as are her accomplishment against the odds, of her success against America's social machines. I see why Harvard's former president, Gay, felt compelled to steal from Dr. Swain. Dr. Swain seems like everything Gay isn't.

The simple truth is that Dr. Carol Swain is the one person in America who has the academic and moral standing to call out the kind of frauds and justifications that have brain-rotted Harvard and our elite institutions. Harvard and big academia are today poisoned by a myopic obsession with titles and a reckless disregard for substance, all in the name of identity politics and fragile egos that struggle to survive in the real world outside the green ivy of theory. Why does America kneel to their self-important supremacy? Here, Dr. Carol Swain has repeatedly shown the academic integrity and honesty to call them out.

— **Chanel Rion,** Harvard graduate and anchor, *Fine Point*, One America News

Acknowledgments

Proverbs 24:6 states "For by wise counsel you will wage your own war, And in a multitude of counselors there is safety (NKJV).

INDEED, THERE ARE MANY PEOPLE WHO HELPED ME DEAL with the unexpected emotions and practicalities surrounding the plagiarism scandal and other life challenges. First, I would like to thank the members of Nancy Dunn's Sunday School Class, the faithful prayer warriors at Forest Hills Baptist Church, and my personal prayer groups for their unwavering support. Their prayers and words of encouragement have sustained me during challenging times. Secondly, I am indebted to my editor and friend, Mike Towle, who is a one-man editor, production team, coordinator, and publisher for Be the People Books. Mike's extensive experience in the world of publishing and his insights have proven invaluable over the years.

My former attorneys, Robert Kleinman, Chase Neely, Joseph Lackey, and Gavin Dwyer worked hard on my behalf. In addition, Tom Fitton and Paul Orfanedes of Judicial Watch gave me wise advice, as did other friends such as former Ohio Representative Bob McEwen,

Acknowledgments

Professor James Blumstein, Robert Shillman (Dr. Bob), and Christopher Schorr. Dr. Arthur Laffer has become a faithful friend and mentor; he always has wise advice and an anecdote for the occasion. Jules Wortman is a tenacious publicist who initially volunteered her time to help me with *The Adversity of Diversity*. Lastly, Donna Willis, in the words of Forrest Gump, has become my "best good friend." Her humor and commonsense insights about world events help keep me grounded.

Preface

OSCAR WILDE FAMOUSLY SAID THAT, "Imitation is the sincerest form of flattery that mediocrity can pay to greatness." As a creative thinker and visionary, I have had plenty of ideas swiped, starting in graduate school and continuing today in projects and other areas where I interact with people who are grasping for ideas. Sometimes in the past I have been flattered, and today I am honored when my ideas in social media posts find their way into articles and news commentary. I was not, however, thrilled to learn on December 10, 2023, that Harvard University's then-President Claudine Gay had just been busted for plagiarizing the work of numerous scholars—me included—starting back in 1997, when she was a graduate student writing her own PhD dissertation, at Harvard. (See my commentary and excerpts from Gay's dissertation abstract and introduction in Appendix D starting on page 98.)

Plagiarism, which is taking other people's work and presenting it as your own, used to be considered a serious breach of academic integrity. It could get a student kicked out of college or failed for a semester, or it could result in the firing of a journalist or an exposed scholar. Plagiarism can take different forms. It can be the theft of someone else's ideas or concepts, or the copying of their words, sometimes verbatim, sometimes paraphrased, but often unattributed, uncited, and/or unsourced. Most brazenly of all, the "borrowed" content is presented without quotation marks inserted before and after the sentences or paragraphs that were copied word for word, i.e., verbatim.

As I will discuss later, Gay took verbatim sentences and words from *Black Faces, Black Interests: The Representation of African Americans in Congress*, my award-winning first book published in 1993 and updated in 1995. More seriously than that, however, she used my book to set up a "strawman" for her own research agenda without acknowledging the source of her "brilliant" award-winning dissertation idea that helped set the stage for her career. Gay violated traditional academic norms of what is considered acceptable in scholarly research. For decades she got away with it until a tipster started contacting journalists about the problems with her scholarly record. Eventually, a pair of investigative reporters and a tenacious reporter with the *Washington Free Beacon* found that Gay had allegedly committed nearly fifty acts of plagiarism in her published works, starting with her prize-winning dissertation.

It seems as if Harvard's doctorate-review committee had failed in 1997 to properly supervise the work of a student who was often described as "brilliant." What I know about the standards usually required to earn a PhD at a tier-one university has caused me to question whether Claudine Gay has met the standards required to be referred to as "Dr. Gay." There is a process, or at least used to be one, for earning a Doctorate in Philosophy. It once required original, pathbreaking work, successfully defended before a committee who put you through the grinder before bestowing the title upon the recipient who was then rewarded with a wine and cheese celebration to mark the occasion.

Back in the mid-1990s, when Claudine Gay was a graduate student at Harvard, the concepts referred to as "Diversity, Equity, and

Inclusion" (DEI) had not yet been integrated into the vernacular of American thought and culture, but "political correctness" and speech codes were on the rise. The future of race-based affirmative action was top of mind for most people in academia and at elite K-12 academies. Elite universities across the country were seeking talented minorities, while administrators expressed great concern that a conservative Supreme Court might do irreparable harm to society by ending affirmative action.

The Shape of the River: Long-Term Consequences of Considering Race in College and University Admission was coauthored in 1998 by William G. Bowen and Derek Bok, former presidents of Princeton and Harvard, respectively. It came out after Claudine Gay was finishing her doctoral work at Harvard, and after national criticism of affirmative action was hitting a crescendo. Opponents of affirmative action were pointing out that the policy was unconstitutional (it indeed was, and now officially is) and unfair to white and Asian student applicants whose higher grade-point averages and test scores were routinely rejected by colleges and universities in favor of lower-performing minority applicants. Bowen and Bok, though, wrote as if it were their civic mission to defend affirmative action and its politically correct nature, insisting that without it our nation would soon be devoid of minority leaders.

Bingo! Along comes Claudine Gay, the offspring of Haitian immigrants, whose growing reputation as the "Brilliant Claudine Gay" dating back to her undergraduate days (at Princeton and Stanford, respectively) made her the perfect poster girl for whatever the forerunner for DEI was called in those days. Left out of the story was the fact that this Haitian immigrant was the scion of one of the wealthiest families in dirt-poor Haiti. It was also no secret that elite colleges and universities often used affirmative action to give a disproportionate leg up to the offspring of immigrants who dominated their entering classes. Black descendants of slaves or students with my profile of hailing from poverty were in short supply among the entering classes. It was about pedigree, baby! Who is going to fit in better here?

Preface

The Gay Affair is actually as much about DEI and affirmative action, and their respective and connective failures, as it is about Gay's perceived serial plagiarism and Harvard's oversight, neglect, or unwillingness to properly vet her dissertation that we now know needed to be fixed before it was approved, published, and won a Harvard University award. Although she had the perfect profile and pedigree, I believe Gay was in over her head by the time she enrolled in Harvard's political science doctorate program. A key part of that evidence was her inability, laziness, or defiance of principle to follow certain stringent yet simple rules of scholarship that she should have learned at Phillips Exeter Academy. Even though I never attended high school, I learned somewhere—either in my high school equivalency course or at the community college where I earned my first degree—to cite sources and give proper attribution to the work of others, using citations, footnotes, quotation marks, and block quotes. Most college-bound high school students have learned the basics in middle school, and it gets reemphasized in courses where term papers and theses are assigned. Anyone can make a mistake, but where there is a pattern across years and across works, it becomes clear that something more serious is taking place.

Here is my contention. In addition to verbatim theft of sentences and word expressions, Claudine Gay used ideas in *Black Faces* to frame her dissertation even though she offered an opposing conclusion meant to counter the provocative conclusions of my work that was impacting real world decision-making. Most egregious was the audacity of my research to question the sacred claim that only black members of Congress could represent black people. There was a proper way to take me down. Claudine Gay should have acknowledged, challenged, and refuted my claims with her own original research. Presenting quantitative data that has been called into question by other scholars should have been addressed during the tenure process. Likewise, the problems with her dissertation should have been flagged by her dissertation committee.

In Appendix B (which starts on page 64), you have an opportunity

Preface

to read a long letter of legalese that Claudine Gay's attorney, Neil Roman, sent my attorneys outlining their arguments and warning me of the dire consequences if I persisted in seeking a legal remedy from the school in regard to what I believed to be Gay's plagiarism of my work. Harvard University had hired a third-party firm that referred my attorney back to Neil Roman's letter I referenced above. Roman is one of the top copyright attorneys in the nation. I would soon learn from experts in the field that copyright law has never been fully tested in academia and that it was not written for cases like mine. Plagiarism itself is an ethical problem. It is not a crime or a misdemeanor. The only policing that takes place at most institutions must come from administrators and general counsels who take academic integrity seriously and have made a commitment to police their students, faculty, and administrators so that high-profile breaches don't merely get slaps on the wrist. As I would soon learn, copyright law does not protect one from the theft of ideas. Copyright law protects copyright holders. The sentences and passages pilfered from *Black Faces, Black Interests*, were described as *de minimis* (minimal) and old-fashioned plagiarism was reimagined by Harvard as being simply "duplicative language." Stolen words and sentences were described as fair use.

Roman's April 23 letter contained a lot of blustering and a clear warning if I persisted in filing a legal complaint against Ms. Gay. After receiving the letter, I contacted Vanderbilt Law School Professor Jim Blumstein, a former colleague and an eminent law professor who has argued and won cases before the U.S. Supreme Court. Professor Blumstein read the letters from Roman and Harvard's attorney Allison Stein, along with my case materials. We had a long lunch where he offered me some wise advice in the form of an analogy I could understand. Professor Blumstein used Hamas's October 7, 2023 attack on Israel and the resulting wipeout of Gaza. Hamas sent a few thousand fighters over the Gaza-Israel barrier and attacked innocent Israelis. Israel responded with a show of force that wiped out much of Gaza. Blumstein's point was crystal clear: Never pick a fight with an enemy who can wipe you out. (You can read my compete legal complaint in Appendix C starting on page 82.)

Preface

Walking away from suing Harvard was difficult. My personality is not one that allows me to easily back down, especially when millions of Americans were cheering me on and a few hundred had sent donations to GiveSendGo (www.givesendgo.com), the conservative alternative to GoFundMe. Bullies should never get off easily. Harvard Corporation has become the Big Dog in the pack who has no qualms about ripping apart anyone who dares come against it. Once an institution has accumulated an endowment that exceeds fifty billion dollars, it might not be too interested in doing the right thing.

I take a risk by telling my story and releasing documents for public consumption. I have a more noble purpose than merely exposing Harvard University. I hope this book will make a real-world difference that will impact other institutions of higher education. Nothing would please me more than to see Harvard and similar institutions of higher education rediscover and re-embrace academic integrity and high standards for scholarly research. World-class Harvard University does the nation an injustice when it lowers standards for some people while coming down hard on others because its leaders lack the courage to fight for values that once were universally accepted in higher education.

Letting Harvard off the legal hook was a difficult decision. After much prayer, reflection, and consultation with experts and friends such as Blumstein, I closed the GiveSendGo (www.givesendgo.com) account which had netted around $30,000 toward my legal expenses, and I instructed my lawyers to close my case even though the legal complaint was finished and ready to be filed in federal court. You can see the letters (Appendix B starting on page 64) and read the complaint (Appendix C starting on page 82). I got cold feet after learning from the experts that under copyright law, the loser pays, meaning that I might have ended up paying for Harvard's high-priced lawyers, some of whom reportedly bill at $1,000 an hour, as well as my own legal team billing at a more modest $350 per hour. My lack of adequate financial resources played a key role in my decision-making. The last thing I

Preface

wanted as a senior citizen was to file a case, lose, and end up using my retirement and social security check to pay off Harvard's attorneys.

Let's be clear! I hold no bitterness or unforgiveness toward Claudine Gay. I see her as a victim and a beneficiary of a system that picks and chooses winners and losers. If at any point along the way, Claudine Gay had picked up the phone to call me or sent an apology, I am certain that I would not be publishing this book. I decided to tell my story because what happens at Harvard affects the entire world. If Harvard downplays and dismisses academic integrity standards of conduct, it will most certainly ripple through other institutions, eventually affecting K-12 education at institutions that once held their students to high standards. The crooked system that exists elevates people and puts them in positions where they don't belong. That system needs to be disrupted.

In this book, I add my voice to those of the disruptors.

— **Dr. Carol M. Swain**
December 2024

THE GAY AFFAIR

CHAPTER 1

The Gay Resignation

EXACTLY ONE YEAR PRIOR TO THIS BOOK'S RELEASE DATE (January 2, 2025), Claudine Gay resigned as president of Harvard University, citing racial animus among the factors forcing her into that position. The timing of this book's release is not a coincidence. It was a decision on my part to turn the one-year anniversary of Gay's resignation into a red-letter date to commemorate (without praise or glee) her serial plagiarism of other people's sentences, paragraphs, and original ideas, such as the glaring breaches of academic integrity found in her 1997 prize-winning Harvard University PhD dissertation that she defended before a Harvard committee about a quarter-century earlier.

Until more corrections are done on her PhD dissertation, she will always be Claudine Gay to me. Calling her Dr. Gay is a bridge too far to traverse. The title of Doctor of Philosophy is meant to be conferred after a student has conducted and successfully defended pathbreaking work before a dissertation committee composed of faculty experts in the field. Gay's dissertation, while successfully defended, fails the academic integrity test on a number of fronts, including questions about the statistical modeling she used to support her conclusions.[1] (See my commentary and excerpts from Gay's dissertation abstract and introduction in Appendix D starting on page 98.)

The Gay Affair

Many suspect Gay was forced by Harvard Corporation's board to resign without making a ruckus. Her "voluntary" resignation for the good of the University was a better look not only for her, but also for Harvard University, which was being pummeled by Congress, the media, and the watching world. As is always the case when race is involved, her public troubles were met with allegations of racism. "Civil rights activist Rev. Al Sharpton . . . described Gay's resignation as 'an assault on the health, strength, and future of diversity, equity, and inclusion.'"[2]

The resignation saved the university, which falls under the auspices of Harvard Corporation, the pain of having to plow its way through what most assuredly would have been a messy, litigious battle if she had filed suit against the University. The question arises: Why cut her the slack? I will explain the apparent reasoning. Gay wasn't just any black faculty member; she has been described as a member of the Haitian aristocracy who graduated from Phillips Exeter Academy and then went to Stanford University for her bachelor's degree after a brief stint at Princeton University. Gay's pedigree made her exactly the kind of black person the Ivy League institutions welcome onto their campuses. As a Harvard PhD student, Gay was frequently described by fellow political scientists as "brilliant." When I first learned of her during my tenure at Princeton University, it was because excited colleagues wanted me to know all about the "brilliant" black student at Harvard University. Much was made of the fact that she did statistical modeling.

Gay became the cat's meow in political science and was hailed as if she were the Second Coming of Christ. By all appearances, Gay was beloved by Harvard insiders. The proud school embraced pride, joy, and historical precedent as its reward for making her the first black person, regardless of gender or gender identity, to serve in the coveted position of thirtieth president of Harvard University. Firing Gay would have been a major public-relations faux pas for a school with a bonkers-high self-esteem that had set a speed record in promoting her into the presidency, only to see her end up serving the shortest presidential tenure in school history.

In the weeks leading up to her resignation, Gay suffered the indignity of being accused of plagiarism as well as misfiring badly in dealing with (she didn't) campus antisemitic activism and threats of genocide against Jewish people. Her inevitable downfall started before her disastrous testimony before a Congressional committee investigation of antisemitism on Harvard's campus. Her tone-deaf testimony, coupled with a plagiarism scandal, essentially doomed her chances of a glorious career as the esteemed university's top dog.

Plagiarism accusations in detail were first reported by a pair of investigative journalists. Their specialty was, and is, sniffing out cases of plagiarism among higher-ups in higher education. This was part of their reporting, generally, on malfeasance in academia. Theirs is a reporter's beat that has kept Christopher Rufo and Christopher Brunet busy, as there is plenty of malfeasance and mischief to go around in higher education.

Zeroing in on Gay and Harvard University might have been for Rufo and Brunet what Watergate was for Woodward and Bernstein. The two intrepid scribes cited numerous instances in which Gay, while at Harvard researching and writing her 1997 PhD dissertation, had allegedly copied and used material gleaned from the published works of others. Essentially all of this was reportedly done without attribution or permission. Even quote marks, deemed an absolute must for material quoted verbatim from someone else's published work, were in absentia.

Aaron Sibarium, of the *Washington Free Beacon*, has conducted investigative reporting that amplified the extent of Gay's pilfering from other scholars. Sibarium cited that as of January 1, 2024, a total of eight of Gay's authored works had been found to contain plagiarism.[3] Those works, according to the *Beacon* as reported by the *Washington Post*, accounted for a total of forty-seven instances of alleged plagiarism spread among Gay's 1997 dissertation, a 2001 working paper, five journal articles she had published while a professor at Stanford and Harvard, and a 1993 essay she penned for *Origins* magazine.[4]

One of those "other scholars" whose published work was pilfered by Gay for her dissertation was me. In terms of word count, her thievery of my work was not overwhelming, but in terms of stolen core ideas, conclusions, and original, innovative scholarship, it was quite substantial. So, how do I characterize my reaction to something like that, when it feels like your home has been ransacked from attic to basement? That entailed a work in recovery progress for me encompassing several months. A year later, it remained a massive bee sting with telltale signs of swelling that has not completely faded away.

Being plagiarized by Claudine Gay is not a source of flattery. I believe it damaged me professionally (which I will explain later) and personally after the dastardly deed came to life and turned everything upside down for a few intense months. Luckily, I was able to regain my bearings and get my life back on track.

When it comes to the Gay affair, it matters little that Claudine and I do not know each other. It is possible I have met her somewhere along the line. She was not so fascinating that any chance meeting left me eager to dig into her brilliant work. After publishing *Black Faces, Black Interests,* my research interests moved in a different direction. That is why I was not aware until December 2023 of how much my work inspired her.

What I learned from her dissertation and early articles on Black representation was that she had used my work to set up a strawman for the work she would publish that sought to counter my findings. There is absolutely nothing wrong in challenging and building upon the published works of other scholars. The proper way to do this is to lay out the other scholar's objectionable findings and then meticulously proceed to dissect them with counterarguments and data to demonstrate the shortcomings of the research. One can also build upon and expand other scholars' work. What is not acceptable is to take the other scholar's conclusions and use them as the basis for your "original" research question and pretend that you were clever enough to come up with the problem. This is not plagiarism in the traditional sense, but it is an unethical theft of ideas that could be more serious than the verbatim theft of random sentences and paragraphs. Both of these violations occurred with my research.

Given the attention my work on congressional representation received, it baffles me how or why Gay's review committee never addressed the matter. We would later learn that Gay's dissertation even plagiarized language from the acknowledgments section of Jennifer Hochschild's dissertation written decades earlier. No matter, Gay's dissertation committee at Harvard approved the dissertation and gave it the highest prize for a social science dissertation. This should leave you scratching your head, but it makes me suspect that when your first name is "Brilliant," and your skin is black, white professors are not going to look too closely at your work.

Gay's choice to resign in early January 2024, instead of waiting to be fired, served her well, just as it did the school. It spared her the hassle and legal expense of fighting the fight (or the ignominy of stooping to plead to keep her job) to avoid being fired, and it kept her in good graces with the school. In turn, Harvard officials, at least publicly, chose not to side with the choir of Gay accusers on the plagiarism issue. The school did, however, green–light a probe into Gay's reported acts of plagiarism once they were reported by the *New York Post*, although the impartiality of the investigation was in question. That is because the investigation was headed by William Lee, a former senior fellow of Harvard Corporation (the University's highest governing body) and at the time a senior partner at WilmerHale, the prestigious law firm chosen by the school to investigate Gay's case. That's keeping it all in the family. Although Lee relinquished his position at Harvard Corporation in 2022, he "has continued to exert significant influence among Harvard's top leadership, including senior administrators, members of the Corporation and his successor, Senior Fellow Penny S. Pritzker," reports the *Harvard Crimson*, the school's student newspaper.[5]

A well-respected law professor, requesting anonymity, told the *New York Post* that Harvard's decision to hire Lee's law firm to investigate Gay following her resignation lacked the appearance of justice. Lee's role at the university, the *Post* reported, quoting the law professor, gave WilmerHale "a tremendous advantage. He's a major figure in the law firm and was a major figure in the corporation." Lee, however, denied there was a conflict.[6]

As it turns out, Harvard Corporation would eventually vote unanimously to clear Gay of any wrongdoing. It was a decision that swiftly drew the chagrin of New York Congresswoman Elise Stefanik, herself a Harvard graduate. She had chaired the Congressional committee that conducted the December 2023 hearing during which Gay gave her self-destructive testimony, for which, ironically, Lee had prepared her.

"The Harvard Corporation actively worked to cover up the negligence and failures of Harvard University, doubling down in defense of its corrupt leadership," Stefanik told the *Post*. "In fact, instead of protecting Jewish students and removing Claudine Gay, former Harvard Corporation Board Senior Fellow William Lee lined the pockets of his law firm WilmerHale, [hired] to defend the former Harvard president's history of serial plagiarism and antisemitism. A reckoning is occurring; our robust congressional investigation will continue to expose the institutional problems plaguing our most elite colleges and universities and deliver needed accountability to the American people."[7]

As for Gay's presumed innocence or guilt regarding the charges of plagiarism?

"The evidence was as plain as a red barn in a snowy field that Gay had appropriated the work of others and passed it off as her own," said Peter Wood, president of the National Association of Scholars, quoted at mindmatters.ai.[8]

It wasn't just Gay herself being questioned about her plagiarism and how or why she had gotten away with it all these years. As opined at the *Guardian*, it came across as "Gay more than anyone should have known better, (but) it seems unfair that she should be the one to take the fall when her errors were missed by the institutions that published her—not least the Harvard PhD committee that awarded her the Toppan prize for the best political science dissertation in 1998."[9] In its efforts to downplay allegations of Gay's plagiarism, Harvard described it as merely "duplicative language without appropriate attribution."[10]

The Gay Resignation

Harvard not only held off denouncing or punishing Gay, but it also slipped a cushion beneath her fall from grace by providing her a golden parachute. That was in the form of a return to a professorship, still at Harvard, that entailed a demotion to the tune of a reportedly robust $900,000-a-year salary. Not a shabby wage for someone who apparently had taken a few dozen shortcuts years earlier on her way to crossing the finish line to grab her doctorate sheepskin. Okay, so her self-esteem, reputation and pride took a hit, as did Harvard's esteemed status to some degree, but other than that let's call it a win-win for Harvard and Gay. Most of the other victims plagiarized by Gay were ideologically aligned and were quick to announce that her actions were fine with them. Some corrections were made, but I am not aware of any that related to her inappropriate theft of my ideas and words. As I mentioned earlier, she has never called me to offer an apology or an explanation. Had she done so, you would not be reading this book.

Harvard's board "had a month and a half to get ahead of this scandal," journalist Jonathan Bailey, also a plagiarism consultant, said, according to the *Guardian*. "I also feel pretty confident that if they had started from the word go, hired an outside expert, made it a transparent process and highlighted the details, they could've gotten ahead of this."[11]

This Gay/Harvard story continued to track with new developments right up until the time I went to publication with this book, and certainly beyond. I was in the middle of writing my preface I saved it for last when I learned that less than a month earlier Gay had been honored with an award for "Leadership and Courage," bestowed on her during a September 2024 assembly by members of the Harvard Black Alumni Society. So there you have it; in this topsy-turvy world of wrong is right and right is wrong, Gay's resignation amidst her "controversial response to antisemitism and the plagiarism allegations"[12] (This is a good thing?) became the gift to herself that keeps on giving. That's if we also count the near-million-dollar annual salary she is now pulling down for who knows how long—

five years, ten, or twenty more years perhaps?—with her still safely ensconced, coddled, and employed at Harvard.

This is one heck of a benefit we can attribute to the DEI program at Harvard. Plus her fellow Harvard Black alumni are thrilled for her:

"This reunion—all these people who were expressing all this support for her—they were all there. Celebrating her, and clapping for her, and cheering her on," said Monica M. Clark, president of the Harvard Black Alumni Society, referring to the September 28 assembly. Thomas G. Stewart, another Harvard alumnus, chimed in, "She's humble, she's smart, she's—fortunately—someone that still is affiliated with the University, and has pledged her support to it to her dying day."[13]

Isn't this just lovely? Below is a slightly edited and abbreviated version of a video commentary I posted on social media within hours after I learned of Gay's alumni award. I can't help myself. This is a good example of my spontaneous off-the-cuff—but brief—social media commentaries I like to offer my thousands of followers when I get riled up. Sometimes, I tweet-storm on X. Here goes:

"I'm old enough to remember when Black people celebrated Black excellence. In the case of Claudine Gay, there is no Black excellence to celebrate. It tells me a lot about at least some black alumni of Harvard when they are willing to cheer and celebrate someone who has been disgraced (and should be shamed) because of the plagiarism and the poor leadership of a Harvard University leader during the attacks on Jewish students. It tells me that Harvard University may not be selecting the right kind of students. I would hope that black students who graduate from Harvard University would be people of character; these would be people who celebrate excellence; these would be people who would want to be leaders, not just of other black people, but for the world at large. I believe in Black excellence, and I hope that you do too."[14]

CHAPTER 2

A 'Plagiaritis' Pandemic?

As the new year dawned with the arrival of 2025, it was evidently safe to say that the spread and severity of COVID cases had calmed significantly since its peak from early 2020 well into 2021. What we now have, though, at least in the world of academia and authorship, is a different type of pandemic. It is one that is a much-lower grade of contagion and certainly less of a health risk than COVID, but still lurks as a threat to scholarly integrity.

I'm talking about the infectious virus of "plagiaritis," which seems to be metastasizing, especially for immunity-deficient college presidents. Those most at risk are those public figures whose published work is now being subjected to a new level of scrutiny, even years after publication. These second-tier probes and careful examinations—which might already be a "witch hunt"—are not coming from review boards vetting the work of PhD aspirants but from investigative journalists and other plagiarism experts with technological tools better equipped or programmed to spot such purloined prose, specifically in published works. It just takes the willingness and know-how of where to look. In today's environment, anyone at any time might discover that twenty-five years ago, they omitted a citation or forgot to include quotation marks. For honest scholars, it would be isolated events that would shock and embarrass them even as they offered apologies for a transgression that everyone was taught how to avoid in high school or college.

Gay is not alone. Other high-profile alleged plagiarists are popping up, to include the most recent vice president of the United States and runner-up to Donald Trump in the 2024 presidential election. Kamala Harris, like the Harvard Black Alumni Society mentioned earlier, no doubt also believes in Black excellence (even if she didn't demonstrate it much during her four years as Joe Biden's vice president or during her failed presidential campaign sprint to the finish). Harris made it to about halfway through October before her own alleged case of "plagiaritis" was pulled out of mothballs. I'm referring to Harris's 2009 book *Smart on Crime*, which, apparently, was not so smart on avoiding plagiarism. She wrote it while California's attorney general.

Written in collaboration with Joan O'C Hamilton, whose front-cover, small-type credit removes her from anonymous "ghostwriter" status (as she is usually described), *Smart on Crime*'s perceived problems pertinent to possible plagiarism were first reported October 14 by Rufo. Based on a dossier compiled by noted Austrian plagiarism hunter Dr. Stefan Weber and detailing *Smart on Crime*'s literary shortcomings, Rufo, writing on Substack, said, "As we have discovered in this exclusive report, another element appears to exist within Kamala Harris's rhetorical universe: plagiarism. . . .

"Harris's book contains more than a dozen 'vicious plagiarism fragments.' Some of the passages (Weber) highlighted appear to contain minor transgressions—reproducing small sections of text; insufficient paraphrasing—but others seem to reflect more serious infractions, similar in severity to those found in Harvard president Claudine Gay's doctoral thesis."[15]

Rufo referenced five somewhat lengthy passages in Harris's book that were particularly problematical, including an unattributed verbatim segment lacking quote marks from an NBC News report; a significant portion of a John Jay College of Criminal Justice press release not cited and without quote marks despite being almost all verbatim;

and two paragraphs lifted from or cited in Wikipedia ("long considered an unreliable source," Rufo rightfully points out) and treated in a similar unattributed, unmarked manner.[16]

Things got stickier when the *New York Times* stuck its nose into the Harris-related fray, publishing a follow-up piece that came across as more determined to build its case against whistleblower Rufo's admittedly right-leaning perspective (and his opposition to "diversity, equity, and inclusion [DEI]" programs) than to address the matter at hand—did Harris plagiarize or not? (Consider the *Times*'s headline: "Conservative Activist Seizes on Passages from Harris Book.")

In its followup review of *Smart on Crime*, the *Times* "found that none of the passages in question took the ideas or thoughts of another writer, which is considered the most serious form of plagiarism." The *Times* also reached out to plagiarism consultant Jonathan Bailey, *Plagiarism Today* website director, to review several questionable *Smart on Crime* pages and comment on them. Plagiarism or not? Well, of course not. Gotta protect Democratic presidential "nominee" Harris leading up to the November 5 election (which she lost, handily, to Donald Trump). Bailey, the *Times* reported, "said . . . that his initial reaction to Mr. Rufo's claims was that the errors were not serious, given the size of the document. 'This amount of plagiarism amounts to an error and not an intent to defraud,' (Bailey) told the *Times*, adding that Mr. Rufo had taken relatively minor citation mistakes in a large amount of text and tried to 'make a big deal of it.'"[17]

Actually, it did become a big deal a day later after Bailey had seen the extent of Rufo's reporting, to include the five lengthy, lifted passages. Bailey realized the *Times* reporters covering the Rufo story had not been given a more complete sampling of the book's areas of concern to pass along for him to review. Subsequently, Bailey wrote on his X (Twitter) account, that his quotes were based on "information provided to me by the (three *Times*) reporters," and that he had not done a full analysis of the book.[18] Fair enough.

Seeing this report, Rufo took off the gloves and also went to X to throw some punches of his own.

The Gay Affair

"The *New York Times* is lying about my plagiarism story, and I have the receipts to prove it," Rufo posted and, as the *New York Post* furthermore reported, via yahoo.com, "accused the *Times* of having 'deliberately withheld' the full analysis authored by Weber (Rufo had given the Weber dossier, "which contained 18 allegations of varying severity" to the *Times*) to minimize the extent of the scandal. When he asked the *Times* 'politely for a correction,' the editor, Mary Suh, 'had nothing but excuses,' Rufo said."[19]

If Harris had any solace in all this, it's that her "boss," Biden, had years earlier gotten caught up in a thicket of his own while navigating his way through a similar dilemma loaded with plagiarism accusations. That was back in 1987, when he was first trying to run for president. Biden at the time admitted to both the plagiarism and his exaggeration of his academic record before dropping out of the race.[20]

When I was in the middle of authoring this book, in autumn 2024, it was reported by the *Daily Wire* that University of Maryland President Darryll J. Pines and coauthor Liming Salvino had composed a dubious paper published in 2002 that only set off alarms present day, more than twenty years later. Their article contained a significant amount of material (reportedly about 1,500 words of their final 5,000-word composition) lacking attribution while closely matching content published and last updated six years earlier on a tutorial website by a college student in Australia. To add insult to insult, Pines and Salvino apparently couldn't resist plying their plagiarism trade once more. Four years later, in 2006, they produced a second peer-reviewed piece that reused much of the same content they had swiped from the student, Joshua Altmann, the first time around.[21] Lesson still not learned.

"Pines, a rocket scientist and diversity activist, does not appear to have made any changes to Altmann's work except removing some sentences and Americanizing the Australian's British spelling (turning 'analyse' to 'analyze,' e.g.)," says Luke Rosiak, writing for dailywire.com. "Pines's systematic editing of British words suggests he did copy the language, but deliberately manipulated Altmann's text to look like his own. The finding of significant past plagiarism comes after Pines (in

September 2024) presented what he said was 'faculty research' defending a pro-Palestine rally planned for October 7, but which actually came from ChatGPT."[22] Note the *Daily Wire*'s subhead that ran with this story: "Revelation Comes Weeks after Darryll Pines claimed AI-Generated Text as 'Faculty Scholarship.'"

The growing roster of college presidents doubling as accused plagiarists includes retired Army Lieutenant General Bob Caslen, a West Point graduate who years later would serve as superintendent and president of the US Military Academy. Not long after retiring from the army, Caslen in 2019 accepted an offer to become president of the University of South Carolina. His presidency there lasted two years. He stepped down after he failed to acknowledge that a lengthy, inspirational portion near the end of a commencement address he gave to graduating seniors had been taken verbatim from elsewhere. That elsewhere was a speech that retired Admiral William H. McRaven had given some seven years earlier while chancellor at the University of Texas System. "I was searching for words about resilience in adversity and when they were transcribed into the speech, I failed to ensure its attribution," an apologetic Caslen wrote to McRaven. "I take full responsibility for this oversight."[23]

Caslen wasn't yet out of the woods at that 2021 USC commencement ceremony, however. Several minutes later, in bringing the ceremony to an end, the former West Point commandant turned to the graduates, asked them to move the tassels on their caps from one side to the other, and declared to them, "It's now my honor and privilege to officially congratulate you as the newest alumni from the University of California."[24] Wrong school—missed it by about three thousand miles.

Keep the line moving. Stanford University President Marc Tessier-Lavigne resigned his position at the Palo Alto, California, school in 2023. He did so after he was ruled responsible for the appearance of manipulated scientific data in his research, although the circumstances in his case were somewhat convoluted. In short, he was at fault, or maybe he wasn't. Portions of the research work Tessier-Lavigne had delegated to students and postdoctoral researchers had been performed sloppily, to include "inappropriate manipulation of research" and "deficient scientific practices," identified through an inquiry conducted by Stanford's board of trustees. Because Tessier-Lavigne was principal author on five papers that included contributions of the flawed work performed by those subordinates, the buck, and his luck, stopped with him. Furthermore, the board stated in its report that "Tessier-Lavigne took insufficient steps to correct mistakes in the scientific record."[25]

Even then, in announcing his resignation, Tessier-Lavigne tried to distance himself from any wrongdoing, declaring that he had been absolved of "'any fraud or falsification of scientific data' but that 'for the good of the University, I have made the decision to step down as president effective August 31 (2023),'" NBC News reported.[26]

Gay a little more than a year later would follow suit, reluctantly stepping away from what surely had to be her dream job.

As I explain later in this book, I, with the help of a law firm I hired, sent two letters of complaint dated about seven weeks apart (which are included in Appendix B starting on page 64) to Harvard explaining how I had suffered injury and reputational harm from the multiple instances in which Dr. Gay had swiped material from my 1993 book *Black Faces, Black Interests* to buffer her own ideas and conclusions at key points in her dissertation, doing so without attribution or sourcing. She couldn't even take the few seconds needed to insert quote marks in the spots where she re-used my material verbatim.

Harvard officials should have been interested in the harm done to me, rather than threaten me with their lawyers as well as with additional financial loss if I pursued the case against them. They were not interested in doing the right thing. Not only were they interested in protecting her, in my opinion they tried to bully me. Because of that, I felt that I couldn't walk away, and that brought me to writing this book, just to get my story and legal complaint out there, even if I couldn't get it done in court. (You can read my compete legal complaint in Appendix C starting on page 82.) When I now think about Ms. Gay, I think beyond her identified victims and see the faces of millions of young people who will see her as a role model who was taken down because of white racism rather than the true story of her downfall. In some ways, it was white racism that refused to hold her accountable. It was easier to redefine racism than to call a spade a spade. Of all the people she plagiarized, Gay had the misfortune of running afoul of the one person who is not wired to walk away. Harvard University could have saved a lot of time, money, and reputational harm by having a conversation with my lawyers. Who knows? We might have reached a win-win settlement.

CHAPTER 3

Black Sunday

It was Sunday, December 10, 2023. I had just gotten home from Forest Hill Baptist Church's Christmas concert when the phone rang. On the line was Dr. Arthur Laffer, the famed economist, author, and a long-time friend of mine. He is best known for conceiving the "Laffer curve" that he originally drew on a napkin fifty years ago, depicting the relationship between tax rates and revenues. What Dr. Laffer was calling me about that Sunday, though, was not to describe his latest doodle on economic theory nor to ask me what the key points of the sermon had been that morning.

"Carol," he said, "have you heard about this? It's just been reported that Claudine Gay, the president of Harvard University, plagiarized her dissertation, and guess who she plagiarized? You." Before I could gather my thoughts for a response, Dr. Laffer suggested to me that I read what reporter Christopher Rufo had just tweeted, breaking the news that twenty-five years earlier, in 1997, a Harvard doctoral candidate named Claudine Gay had allegedly plagiarized the published works of other authors. Me included. This was the same Claudine Gay—now "Dr." Claudine Gay—who in July 2023 had assumed the presidency of Harvard University amidst much fanfare.

Without the successful defense of a path-clearing, original dissertation that she had executed, there would not have been a Dr. Claudine Gay. She was a superstar. In 1998, she was awarded Harvard's Toppan Award for the best dissertation in political science. Not only did she earn a doctorate, she also was rewarded in the sense that Harvard had checked an important box in her journey up the ladder to what would eventually be the school's presidency. It wasn't just that she had apparently plagiarized other published works—copied verbatim without quote marks or source attribution—it is that she had also "stolen" the verbiage, ideas, and conclusions of other authors; again, me included.

It took a couple of journalists well-versed in investigating academic fraud to succeed in doing what Harvard's hiring board was either unable or unwilling to do when vetting Gay for the school's presidency—uncover Gay's ethical indiscretions. One of those investigative journalists is Rufo. He is a writer, filmmaker, activist and senior fellow at Manhattan Institute, and he has been described as "one of the most effective journalists and filmmakers in the country" (by Tucker Carlson), an "international-class troublemaker and policy advisor on the culture war" (Dr. Jordan Peterson), and "the country's pre-eminent critic of critical race theory" (the *New York Times*).[27] Rufo has emerged as a leader of fair-minded watchdog journalists combing the countryside looking to uncover misdeeds, ethical lapses, blatant hypocrisies, and the like when it comes to hot-button issues ranging from DEI and cancel culture to wokeism and gender ideology—or what we might call the Four Horsemen of the Progressive Apocalypse.

Rufo was one of the first journalists, if not *the* first, to start researching rumors of Gay's plagiarism, which entailed not only using others' ideas and conclusions as if they were her own, but also copying verbatim segments of text of varying lengths without attribution. Citing sources, inserting footnotes, marking verbatim text from elsewhere with quote marks, and rewriting borrowed material in your own words as much as possible—that is called "paraphrasing"—is not rocket science. Nor are they the sorts of things you easily forget while performing the research and then inserting the copyrighted material of others into your work and properly crediting the source. It can be very tedious and slow you down, even interrupting your train of thought and narrative flow. No matter. Persevere, stay disciplined, and resist any inclination to slack off in order to speed things back up. That's how you do it correctly. Apparently, Gay never got that memo, at least not *before* she submitted her dissertation for committee review in 1997.

Another factor to consider when referencing another person's work and putting it into yours is fair use. That is a guiding principle, with legalities attached, which governs how much of another author's particular work you can rightfully insert verbatim into your own work without permission—on top of which users are *still* expected to source and punctuate it properly, using [sic] to denote errors in the original. In such instances the author must insert quote marks around all text used verbatim, as well as include properly formatted sourcing, while being careful to use only a small percentage of another author's work. Fair use is a judgment call case by case based on experience, common sense, and adherence to ethical behavior. With fair use, there is no set percentage demarcation line between what amount is legal to use without permission and what could be a copyright infringement that exposes you to possible legal action. As I have learned, in the case of academia, there have been few cases brought and won, because copyright law was not written to police students and unethical scholars.

It's not hard to follow the rules, written and unwritten, in conforming to proper use of another author's work. It's as easy as remembering (but reckless to forget) to turn off the stovetop when you finish cooking, or to close the garage door when you leave your driveway. High school and college students writing essays and term papers do it all the time. This is Academic/Publishing Ethics 101. Gay possibly was researching and writing while tired late at night, just got lazy, or simply had developed bad habits in high school getting groomed at Phillips Exeter for her high role in society. For whatever reason, sloppiness, a disregard for others, a tendency to take shortcuts, she developed a pattern of borrowing other people's ideas and words. Like a cook working without a recipe, it was a little bit of this and a dab of that, until the concoction was complete. In a society focused on equity and social justice, white faculty scholars were primed to cheerlead and affirm when they should have been asking questions and pushing Gay harder to do it right.

Rufo had company in exposing Gay's deep dive into ethical darkness. Journalist Christopher Brunet, a cohort of Rufo's, had been sleuthing along Gay's trail of occasional sloppy research/writing dating back to around early 2022. That was when he received an anonymous email tip from a source at Harvard that a political science professor at Harvard had engaged in research misconduct regarding their past work in academia. "Once I started tugging at that string, it led me directly to Claudine Gay," Brunet told the *American Conservative* for a story that was published in January 2024.[28]

Brunet had been reporting on academic corruption while writing for Substack before moving on to the *Daily Caller*. It was around that time he received his tip about Gay. Confident that he had the makings of a major story that would blow the lid off of America's oldest and arguably most distinguished and reputable institution of higher learning (Harvard)—and its still-new president—Brunet said he pitched his story idea to his *Daily Caller* editors, only for them to shoot it down.

"They wouldn't run it because it was too much legal risk, which is true, because Harvard, they sic lawyers on the *New York Post*, right, they're quick to sue," Brunet said. "So it was a lot of legal risk and not very much upside."[29]

Soon after receiving that editorial rejection, Brunet departed the *Daily Caller*, although he continued to dig on his own into the Gay/Harvard story while also seeking a landing spot for his investigative story once it was completed. The more he shoveled through the dirt, the more incriminating details he uncovered about Gay's academic background and her work. Much of that laborious research took Brunet through piles of public records. Eventually, Brunet was able to connect with Rufo. Together they co-authored a piece entitled

"Is Claudine Gay a Plagiarist?" published jointly by Substack and New York-based *City Journal*.

"I can look at her scholarly record and see it's not very good," Brunet told the *American Conservative*. "And a lot of it was research done by other people. I just connected all the dots together and put it out in a coherent narrative. . . . I've gotten too many emails to even respond to, dozens of emails from people at Harvard or Harvard alumni, or just random academics, telling me how grateful they are. Just because the world was so unfair with her power, because she was so unqualified and corrupt."[30]

CHAPTER 4

Hamas Fallout Reaches Harvard

GAY RESIGNED HER PRESIDENCY AT HARVARD on January 2, 2024, exactly six months and a day after she had assumed office (on July 1, 2023). That covers 186 days, the shortest presidential tenure in Harvard history. Gay's tumble from grace wasn't just related to her plagiarism in her 1997 PhD dissertation. Calls for her resignation had started earlier in the fall of 2023 when she became embroiled in a controversy concerning student conduct on the Harvard campus.

Following the terrorist attack by Hamas on Israel on October 7, Gay declined to condemn Harvard student groups numbering more than thirty who had published a letter holding Israel "entirely responsible" for the Hamas attack, as described in the *New York Post*.[31] Death threats to Jewish people were also being conveyed. Gay and two other college presidents in early December 2023 were called to testify before the US House Committee on Education and the Workforce about their apparent unwillingness to restrict or punish those engaged in antisemitic behavior on their campuses.

The *Harvard Crimson*, the university's student newspaper, summarized Gay's congressional appearance thusly: "In response to a line of questioning from Rep. Elise M. Stefanik '06 (R-NY), Gay said that calls for genocide of Jewish people would not automatically be in violation of Harvard's code of conduct, instead insisting that it depended on the context. Her response, for which she later apologized, went viral just hours after the hearing, and amplified calls for Gay's resignation."[32] Soon the US House passed a resolution recommending that Gay resign as Harvard president. The uproar calling for Gay's resignation became even more widespread and pronounced after reports surfaced of her plagiarism.

By then, Gay's days as president had seemingly become numbered. Or had they? "After staying silent for a week," the *Harvard Crimson* reported, "the Corporation, Harvard's top governing body, released a statement of unanimous support for Gay, following what they said was 'extensive deliberation.' Gay's position was temporarily secured."[33] Five days later, on December 10, Rufo and Brunet's report about Gay and her plagiarism was published on Substack. That's when my name entered the picture, much to my surprise. Gay had apparently plagiarized ideas and sentences from my book *Black Faces, Black Interests*. As soon as I read her articles and thesis, I recognized it—my work was now "hers." She had used my prize-winning book to frame her dissertation research question and random sentences from the book and an article I published on minority representation. The practice and theme carried over into her early articles where she continued the work occasionally listing *Black Faces* in her bibliography, but not where it would have been expected to appear if she had followed traditional academic practices. Following is a partial accounting of what she took from me, reported by Rufo and Brunet in their article "Is Claudine Gay a Plagiarist?":

> Gay appears to lift material from scholar Carol Swain in at least two instances. In one passage, summarizing the distinction between "descriptive representation" and "substantive representation," she copies the phrasing and language nearly verbatim from Swain's book *Black Faces, Black Interests*, without providing a citation of any kind. In her book, Swain writes:

> "Pitkin distinguishes between 'descriptive representation,' the statistical correspondence of the demographic characteristics … and more 'substantive representation,' the correspondence between representatives' goals and those of their constituents."

Gay's version is virtually the same, with slight modifications to the diction and punctuation:

"Social scientists have concentrated . . . between descriptive representation (the statistical correspondence of demographic characteristics) and substantive representation (the correspondence of legislative goals and priorities)."

Gay's use of Swain's material is a straightforward violation of the university's rule on "verbatim plagiarism," which states that one "must give credit to the author of the source material, either by placing the source material in quotation marks and providing a clear citation, or by paraphrasing the source material and providing a clear citation"—neither of which Gay followed.

Later in the paper, Gay also uses identical language to Swain, without adding quotation marks, as required. "Since the 1950s the reelection rate for House members has rarely dipped below 90 percent," reads Swain's book, which is the same, excepting an added comma, to the language in Gay's dissertation: "Since the 1950s, the reelection rate for incumbent House members has rarely dipped below 90%." According to Harvard's rules, this would be a violation of the policy on "inadequate paraphrase," which requires that verbatim language be placed in quotations.[34]

A side-by-side comparison in the letter my attorneys sent to the Harvard attorneys provided more details of other breaches. (That letter is among other letters included or summarized in Appendix B, which starts on page 64). My contention is that there would not have been a Gay dissertation on black congressional representation had she not read and appropriated ideas from *Black Faces*. (Turn to Appendix A on pages 62-63 to see my own side-by-side charts of Gay's most egregious samples of what I believe to be her acts of plagiarism of my book *Black Faces, Black Interests*.)

Harvard University, by its own policy regarding plagiarism, might agree with my assessment, even if it apparently did not in 1997 when Gay's dissertation slipped through Harvard's vetting process. Consider

25

the opening paragraph to "What Constitutes Plagiarism?" that appears on a Harvard University website: "In academic writing, it is considered plagiarism to draw any idea or any language from someone else without adequately crediting that source in your paper. It doesn't matter whether the source is a published author, another student, a website without clear authorship, a website that sells academic papers, or any other person: Taking credit for anyone else's work is stealing, and it is unacceptable in all academic situations, whether you do it intentionally or by accident" (https://usingsources.fas.harvard.edu/what-constitutes-plagiarism).

Upon resigning from the Harvard presidency, Gay would later play the race card in explaining the impetus behind the push against her will in forcing her removal from office. Blacks get to play that card at any time at the slightest provocation, and, unlike timeouts or a coach throwing a red flag to call for a replay review in football, there is no limit on how many times Blacks can use it. To Blacks who consider themselves entitled because of their race, the race card is always available for any minority with their back against a wall.

"In her resignation," the *Post* reported, "Gay cited how she had been subject to racism since the attacks, writing: 'It has been distressing to have doubt cast on my commitments to confronting hate and to upholding scholarly rigor—two bedrock values that are fundamental to who I am—and frightening to be subjected to personal attacks and threats fueled by racial animus.'"[35]

Not long after I finished my phone conversation with Dr. Laffer on that Sunday back in December 2023, my phone rang again. This time it was a reporter from the *Tennessee Star*, in Nashville, asking me if I knew about the accusations of plagiarism against Gay—I told him I did—and what my reaction was. In the moment, I was willing to give Gay benefit of the doubt. But I also knew I needed to learn more about what Harvard's then-still-president had done years earlier as a doctoral student, with my own copyrighted work being of great interest to me. I had to find out fast because I knew that the *Star* reporter's phone call would soon be joined by calls from others, which is what happened.

Once I got that first tweet out on X (Twitter) to let my followers know that I was aware of what was going on, my next step was to get online and start researching Gay and her work, to include the now-controversial dissertation. It's not like she had copied reams of my work without attribution, but she had stolen enough to presumably help construct her dissertation and to make me feel violated in an academic sense. Whatever free ride she had given herself was in part paid for by me. To me it was analogous to stealing someone else's documentation describing in detail a device they had just created and using the proprietary information and filing for the patent under their name. It might not be an invention worthy of a Nobel Prize, but it's the precious essence to the original inventor's life's work. That's stooping pretty low.

One of the first examples of Gay's work I came across online was an article she had written years earlier on Black congressional representation in the US. Curiously, it cited me in a couple of places and contained no verbatim passages from my work, but it ("The Effect of Black Congressional Representation on Political Participation") was titled similarly to my PhD dissertation, which I had written in 1989 as a doctoral candidate at the University of North Carolina–Chapel Hill. The title of my dissertation: "The Politics of Black Congressional Representation."

In doing my own dissertation research thirty-five years earlier, starting with identifying a topic, the clear expectation was that one has to conduct original research and make a major contribution to a research area. As I stated in the preface, my problem was never a shortage of ideas. I had plenty of topics that interested me, but the issue of minority representation in Congress was the one that fascinated me the most. What was representation? Is it true that only Blacks can represent Blacks? Everyone else seemed to believe this was true, but I was not convinced.

It was my curiosity and desire to answer a burning question that set in motion the chain of events that led to my dissertation, its National Science Foundation funding, and ultimately the pathbreaking work on black congressional representation. It was as simple as that!

The points I made and the questions I raised in my dissertation were strong enough to garner for me that National Science Foundation (NSF) funding of $11,000 for my field research, the sort of NSF award that isn't just given out to anybody. This was not a DEI gift to me. DEI didn't exist then, or at least not in the form it has taken today. Affirmative action did exist and was offering equal opportunity to succeed or fail. It took a few decades for current DEI to become affirmative action on steroids.

I have always felt a constant need to prove myself. Striving for more led me to earn five college and university degrees, early tenure at an Ivy League institution, and three national prizes for my work. My dissertation became the foundation for *Black Faces, Black Interests: The Representation of African Americans in Congress*. It was originally published in 1993, expanded and re-released in 1995, and reprinted again in 2006, by University of America Press. It remains in print. By 1997, *Black Faces* had won three national prizes. At that point, it had not yet been cited in US Supreme Court cases—it eventually would—but it had been cited in lower-court cases.

Remember, too, that it was in 1997 that Claudine Gay defended her doctoral dissertation at Harvard, years after my prize-winning book had been published.

It was after the publication of *Black Faces* when I first experienced attacks from liberal whites and black scholars unhappy with my research findings that ran afoul of the party line. It was a lonely period of my life. Being labeled as a conservative stung. I disappointed some people because I was not what one would expect from a black female who had grown up poor in southwestern Virginia. Had it not been for Gay's poor performance during her congressional testimony when Representative Elise Stefanik mercilessly grilled her about the treatment of Jews on campus and her inability to outright condemn the harassment they were experiencing on a daily basis, the plagiarism might have remained buried for a while longer. I don't know for how long because Gay had intrepid investigators nipping at her heels. Rufo, Brunet, and Aaron Sibarium were doggedly persistent once they got wind of what Gay was alleged to have done. These reporters are the true heroes because they made it their business to expose the wrongdoing.

CHAPTER 5

Plagiarism Déjà Vu

THE GAY CASE WAS NOT THE FIRST TIME that my ideas had been "borrowed" by other scholars without my permission. That takes me back almost forty years, to when I was a graduate student at Virginia Tech University in the 1980s.

Like I mentioned in my preface, I have always been able to see connections that other people often miss. Even today, I have a knack for coming up with ideas that other people find worthy of repeating. It is not uncommon for me to read my words in other people's articles and posts. For example, during the Obama Administration, I was the first to coin the phrase "stealth immigration reform." Later I referred to Gay as a "serial plagiarist" and watched the characterization take flight.

While I was at Virginia Tech, I worked on one of my two master's degrees, which involved lots of classes and term papers. One of the professors with whom I was working accused one of his colleagues—who happened to be the chair of the department—of plagiarizing a paper I had written using the dataset of the professor, who then took the case to the university administration. It placed me in the uncomfortable situation of having to sit in front of a university committee to answer questions about the research paper.

I remember being enormously flattered that a big-name professor would be interested in any of my ideas. At the time, and perhaps now, professors would often argue that if a student took one of their classes, any ideas they originate must have come from the professor teaching the course. This matter was resolved in a manner that resulted in the accused professor—who published an article using ideas in my term paper—leaving the University for greener and more fertile pastures. The professor who brought the charge against him never fully recovered from the incident. I was his research assistant. Years later, I would learn that he felt that the theft of the ideas from my research paper hurt him because it usurped research he had been working on for years. It was a sad situation. For me, I was just a student passing through a graduate program. I was not interested in departmental politics; I just wanted to get my degree and keep moving.

A similar thing happened several years later. This was in the late 1980s while I was finishing my dissertation at the University of North Carolina at Chapel Hill. Shortly after I gave a colloquium at Duke University on my National Science Foundation-funded dissertation, one of the assistant professors in the department decided to embark on a study that was strikingly similar. Not surprisingly, it raised eyebrows around the country among other political scientists who expressed their concern to me. By this time, I had a book contract with Harvard University Press, and I was finishing the dissertation that became the backbone of *Black Faces, Black Interests*. Fortunately, my book was published years before the then-assistant professor, who had started on the similar research path, got his book published. He properly cited my work and even asked me for a book endorsement, which I gave because by then it did not matter. The professor in question did cite my work.

Ironically, his was among the works that Claudine Gay apparently plagiarized in her dissertation, taking even larger chunks of his work, presumably because this professor's conclusions aligned more closely with hers. In so doing, Gay plagiarized the derivative work of a scholar whose research on black representation in Congress closely aligned with my work on black representation. The majority of the scholars whose works were plagiarized by Gay were individuals who were ideologically aligned with Gay. I was not ideologically aligned even though I was a Democrat at the time. I was just interested in becoming the best congressional scholar I could be. My efforts were rewarded when among the prizes I won for *Black Faces* was the D. B. Hardeman Prize given by the Lyndon Baines Johnson Foundation for best book "that furthers the study of the U.S. Congress in the fields of biography, history, journalism, or political science." In addition, I won the Woodrow Wilson Foundation Award for "the best book on government, politics, or international affairs," and I shared the V.O. Key Award for best book on Southern Politics. It would have been impossible for Claudine Gay or her committee members to not have been aware of the connections between our respective works.

REAL RESEARCH IS A REAL BEAR

Conducting original research is hard work. I started my research while in college at a time when we used the Dewey Decimal Classification for library books. Typewriters, yellow legal pads, and five-by-six-inch lined note cards were some of our tools of the trade. It was tedious work, and it required a focus on detail that is not something I am naturally good at doing. I am convinced that I am an undiagnosed ADHD adult. I am a creative, right-brained person who has thrived in a left-brained world. For my dissertation research in the late 1980s, I conducted field research around the country and spent untold hours, mostly in libraries, using microfiche to find information and details for some of the legislative districts I was writing about. (It only takes an hour or two of spooling and scanning through microfiche before nausea starts gathering in your gut, making such antiquated research a tough endurance activity.) I also spent time at the Library of Congress in Washington, DC, to use many of their abundant resources.

I did months of research and travel before coming up with the ideas and thesis that would make *Black Faces, Black Interests* a prize-winning book. Interviews were tape recorded and transcribed. Almost everything had to be done and recorded by hand—neither the Internet nor cell phones nor laptops were around then. My recording tools included the yellow legal pads and white note cards. I used the antiquated resources to conduct original research to develop the ideas that would earn me early tenure at Princeton University. At that time, the Ivy League required a pathbreaking peer-reviewed book as the price of admission to the tenured ranks. Most people failed. I did not! Gay sailed through the tenure process without pathbreaking work or articles of any significance. Standards, I believe, dropped precipitously after the affirmative action debates of the 1990s, when elites closed ranks around preferential treatment for Blacks and Hispanics.

I choose black representation in Congress as a research topic because there were scores of newspaper articles that argued Black representation in Congress would soon end. That's because there were only two remaining majority black districts with white representatives that Blacks could flip and claim. One of these districts was in Newark, New Jersey, and represented by Peter Rodino; the other was in New Orleans, Louisiana, and represented by Lindy Boggs. It was widely believed that as soon as black candidates claimed the two remaining districts, that black power in Congress would diminish because "only Blacks could represent Blacks." Really? I openly wondered if it were true that only Blacks could represent Black interests. Something about that assertion did not sit right with me. My research question essentially asked, *Is it true that only Blacks can represent Black interests?* To answer the question, it was necessary for me to define Black interests and explore the different forms and meanings of representation that became my research topic.

What I did that was unusual was decide to study white and black members of Congress, selecting my cases based on the demographic makeups of the legislative districts. My configurations included black and white representatives of majority Black districts; black and white representatives of majority white districts; and black and white representatives of heterogenous districts where Blacks comprised at least 40 percent of the populace. Instead of focusing solely on voting records, however, my study also involved traveling to districts around the country to not only see what they were doing in terms of how they voted—and the doing was in the details—but also what they were doing day to day in that district (the work that was going on behind the scenes). I was interested in the congressmen's staffs; who did what exactly; the racial composition of their respective staffs; the number and location of district offices; the accommodations for language minorities; and the ease of access. And did they have a *mobile* district office?

My study was original work, and I remember the pressure I felt that came from my desire to meet high standards and to not let down the people who believed and invested in me. My fear was that after I had completed all the travel and collection of data, I would not have anything worthy to report, that there would be nothing from which to build a breakthrough conclusion or even a compelling story to tell. My fear did not subside until I landed the Harvard Press contract for a book manuscript and successfully defended my dissertation. It was never a cakewalk for me. It was hard work and much of that time I was a single mother, and it was very stressful. I knew I needed a home run to achieve my goals.

My work on representation built on the seminal research of Hanna Pitkin, who pioneered the 1967 book *The Concept of Representation* that every serious student of representation cites in their literature reviews. As far as I can tell, Gay never cites Pitkin. However, in one of the places where Gay pilfers from my work, she references the part of the sentence where I refer to Pitkin's definition of descriptive representation. How this omission escaped the Harvard faculty puzzles me. Traditionally, master's and dissertation students in the field of social science had to conduct thorough literature reviews to show how their work was connected to the work of other scholars relevant to the field. When I read Gay's dissertation and articles, I see almost none of this.

Gay's dissertation is one that mastered the art of shortcuts. In too many places, she copied paragraphs and sentences of other scholars rather than write her own narrative. What she brought to the process that was different from what I did in *Black Faces, Black Interests* was quantitative analysis, something that was highly praised among social scientists at the time (late 1990s) and far sexier than the old-fashioned field research and participant observation I engaged in for my study. By the time Gay finished her dissertation, *Black Faces, Black Interests* was creating a stir in voting rights because of my "controversial" conclusions. I argued that political party was more important than the race of a representative and that there was a tradeoff between black descriptive and black substantive representation. That means you could have more black faces in Congress and less Black representation if the strategy for increasing the number of Blacks in Congress meant the loss of seats and power for one's party.

I committed the "unforgivable" sin of arguing that whites could represent Blacks, and Blacks could represent whites. I also shocked people by claiming that white voters would support black candidates and that it was their liberalism and not their race that accounted for their losses in some Democrat districts. These ideas infuriated the liberal left, even though I was a Democrat when *Black Faces* was published. It would be many years later before I gradually transitioned out of the party.

I suspect that Claudine Gay's more palatable ideological alignment led left-leaning political scientists to turn a blind eye to Gay because they needed a high-profile black person to counter my ideas. Had it not been for the controversial nature of my findings in *Black Faces*, I believe it is possible Gay's dissertation committee would have flagged this and advised her to acknowledge and cite my work in her literature review. Her research question is basically a rewrite of a point I made in my concluding chapter.

I reiterate that there is absolutely nothing wrong with challenging the ideas of another scholar or building upon them. What is unconscionable in my view is for someone to take another scholar's ideas without proper attribution and use their work to set up a strawman that you attempt to take apart without an indication of what you are doing and why. In the case of Gay, her work has also been questioned for reasons other than plagiarism. Her quantitative analyses have been deemed as flawed. She has repeatedly rebuffed requests to release her "scientific" data for other scholars to replicate. As much as I am disappointed in Gay, I am more disappointed in the Harvard faculty who clearly held her to a lesser standard by not making her meet rigorous standards before awarding her a prize for a dissertation that was clearly not ready for prime time.

CHAPTER 6

A Legal Remedy

INITIATING LEGAL ACTION AGAINST GAY AND HARVARD wasn't my first thought after I took the call from Dr. Laffer on that Sunday, December 10, 2023. My anger and frustration built up the more I read her published works on black representation. In only one of her articles does she make an attempt, a feeble one at that, to acknowledge my work in an acceptable manner. In addition to Gay's dissertation, the works of hers in which I found similarities with my research included "The Effect of Black Congressional Representation on Political Participation," which I also referenced in chapter 4. Two others I found: "The Effect of Minority Districts and Minority Representation on Political Participation in California," (Public Policy Institute of California, 2001) and "Spirals of Trust? The Effect of Descriptive Representation on the Relationship Between Citizens and Their Government" (*American Journal of Political Science*, 2002). These three peer-reviewed published works were presented as part of her tenure package. Tenure, if lifelong, is a faculty appointment that cannot be removed without cause.

The day after I got the phone call from Dr. Laffer, I got online and started looking for, finding, and reading through her articles on congressional representation, and I was quickly troubled. The entire situation made me profoundly sad. I felt a deep sadness for myself and for Gay because I was certain Harvard was going to fire her and that it was not a good look for Black excellence. I viewed Gay as a victim of a system that had tried to meet quotas for racial and ethnic minorities. Harvard, being Harvard, was positioned to get the best of the lot. Claudine Gay with her world-class education was exactly what institutions were fighting over when recruiting "five-star" students. Again, this was the era of affirmative action and the beginning of the fear among the elites that the courts might end the programs to the detriment of Blacks and Hispanics. Some universities and colleges had administrators who believed that holding students to high standards would mean lily-white campuses.

This attitude takes us back to the subject of diversity, equity, and inclusion (DEI), which has wreaked havoc on society. Affirmative action on steroids. You can learn more about my thoughts on DEI in my 2023 book *The Adversity of Diversity: How the Supreme Court's Decision to Remove Race from College Admissions Criteria will Doom Diversity Programs*. Given Gay's world-class education, she should have been everything that the Harvard faculty imagined her to be when they fast-tracked her, bigly.

This is not uncommon. There has long been an affirmative action push—specifically, the DEI push—to fast-track people of color into positions of power. Harvard, in my estimation, had pushed Gay beyond her limit. That made her either the beneficiary or the victim of the Peter Principle, depending on one's perspective. That refers to the phrase coined in the self-indulgent seventies by authors Raymond Hull and Dr. Laurence J. Peter, whose seminal work, *The Peter Principle* (actually published in 1969, but that's a minor quibble), was a runaway best-seller. It served as one of the published pillars of the era of "me, myself, and I." *The Peter Principle* advanced the theory that all people are subject to a workplace or organizational dynamic in which they eventually are promoted to their level of incompetence. That could describe Claudine Gay's ascent through Harvard's organizational chart all the way to the presidency.

A Legal Remedy

After sadness, then came anger for me as I saw Harvard come out in support of Gay. One of the first things they did was perform semantics gymnastics by trying to re-define plagiarism as "duplicative language." Anger is not a natural emotion for me. In fact, it felt rather strange and unhealthy; Gay was going to get away with blaming racism even after helping herself to the works of others, including mine that had defined my rise as a recognized congressional scholar.

The Gay affair derailed me. At this time in life, I had just resumed work on my memoir after a couple years of dealing with other priorities. But all that was put on hold once again when I was hit with an onslaught of interview requests once word of the Gay plagiarism allegations had gotten out. Plus, it was getting close to Christmas, and I certainly like to celebrate Christmas with family members. I didn't want to spend my time moping around, so as best I could I pushed through what was a difficult time in my life. I took to social media and I started to post Scriptures that I was reading for solace. The reaction was so positive that something that I thought was just a one-time post has become an almost-daily occurrence. It allows me to share myself with the hundreds of thousands of social media followers I have across my media platforms with X being my favorite.

I struggled through the holidays and was feeling better about things and coping well. That was until I heard the news on January 2, 2024, that Gay had resigned as Harvard's president. She in part blamed her plight on racism, claiming she was a victim. That's an odd characterization when you consider how, in resigning, Harvard handed her that plum $900,000 plus-a-year job while demoting her back to the rank of professor, which might be roughly equivalent to reducing in rank a three-star general to bird colonel. For Gay, it was a golden parachute packed into a demotion. Typical DEI-related phooey. Note that Gay had officially risen to the Harvard presidency six months earlier, on July 1, 2023. Ironically, that was just two days after the US Supreme Court had ruled 6-3—in a landmark case (small world: Harvard was one of two defendants in that case) that involved affirmative action—that the use of race-conscious admissions practices was now unconstitutional.

The Gay Affair

This takes me back to my earlier reference to Gay's January 2, 2024, resignation statement in which she mentions how frightening it is "to be subjected to personal attacks and threats fueled by racial animus."[36] It's the "racial animus" phrase that really sticks out.

What's not to dislike about any of this: the idea that a perpetrator can identify herself (or himself) as victim. Consider that sizable almost-seven-figure salary as Gay's own unique form of reparations for the "racial animus" that had befallen her. Gay's resignation was quickly followed by Harvard's own letter, expressing regret for her departure from the presidency. They implied that she (still) was a great scholar and that her resignation was a loss to the spirit and traditions of academia, presumably, the version practiced with true rigor. That made me angry all over again (I know, I'm showing lots of anger here—I'm almost done with that).

That got me to thinking back to a week or two earlier, when I had been approached by a lawyer, Robert Kleinman from Austin, Texas, about working *pro bono* for me to get a lawsuit filed against Gay and Harvard. Remembering this, I contacted Mr. Kleinman and said, "Let's do this." He and his firm wrote the first letter on my behalf to Harvard, a brief and to-the-point letter that established how my book *Black Faces, Black Interests* had been a seminal work on Black representation in Congress, that Gay had plagiarized from it in several instances in her 1997 PhD dissertation, and that I was "entitled to certain rights and remedies arising from the prohibited use of its content." The letter was dated January 3, 2024, the day after Gay's resignation from Harvard. You can read the whole letter, as well as excerpts of others between my attorneys and Harvard's team of lawyers, in Appendix B, which starts on page 64. The January 3 letter was the first "salvo" in a succession of correspondence between me and my attorneys and those attorneys representing Harvard and Gay over a period of about four months.

Two weeks after that first letter went out, on January 17, we heard from Harvard, and I was advised to follow their internal Harvard procedure. Around that time I decided to terminate the agency of Mr. Kleinman and retain Lackey and McDonald because I needed attorneys licensed in Tennessee, and it was not clear to me how the pro bono attorney would work with the hired guns. During this time, none of the big public-interests law firms on the conservative side were interested in going up against Harvard and losing (big time). Much to their credit, however, Tom Fitton and Paul Orfanedes of Judicial Watch gave advice and stayed informed about the progress of the case. Lackey and McDonald was retained because of the firm's local reputation. I needed a firm that could file in federal court and be taken seriously, at least in Tennessee, because from Harvard's perspective, we were probably viewed as country bumpkins akin to the stereotypes of the South found in the legal comedy *My Cousin Vinny*. It was on April 23 that we received two similar letters, one from Gay's attorney, Neil Roman, and the other from Harvard's third-party counsel, Allison Stein. In reading those two final letters, especially the longer one from attorney Neil Roman, it didn't take us long after we started to realize neither one of them was going to offer us a conversation that might lead to a mutually acceptable settlement. Instead, Mr. Roman was going to educate me and my perceived "bumbling" southern attorneys about the intricacies of law. They were also, perhaps, and I am being generous here, trying to avoid taking the retirement funds of a senior citizen. Again, turn to Appendix B in the back that features this exchange of correspondence between January 3, 2024 and April 23, 2024.

The April 23 letter from Neil Roman surprised my lawyers and me. We expected Harvard to engage in a negotiation. Nevertheless, my attorneys encouraged me to continue the lawsuit because they felt that the case had all the makings of one that could be the basis for an expansion of copyright law, given that there were few cases involving academia. By this time, I had growing concerns about rising legal costs. I asked my attorneys, Lackey and McDonald, if they believed in the case enough to work *pro bono* going forward. They declined.

I spoke with other attorneys, including Professor Blumstein, the eminent law professor friend of mine referenced in my preface. Through him and others, I learned that federal copyright law has a loser-pays provision that has no cap on the amount of fees that a judge might impose. I already knew that my legal fees could exceed $250,000 if the case went to trial. My lack of resources was a huge deterrent going forward. Visions of me, a senior citizen, using social security and retirement savings to pay Harvard's big dog lawyers danced in my head. While I was willing to risk losing the case, I was not prepared to use my life savings to pay Harvard's attorneys.

This is another form of trending "lawfare" (warfare fought in courts or by bullying legalese to legally "knock out" an opponent). It is what President-Elect Donald Trump has had to deal with ever since announcing he was running for a second presidential term (successfully as it turns out). Like what happened to him in New York when a left-leaning district attorney and a like-minded judge effectively teamed up to stick Trump with a felony conviction as ridiculous as the Democrat Party is in general. In my case, I didn't trust the legal system once I saw what Harvard's legal representatives sent back to us, and it confirmed for me how clear it was that copyright law was flawed when applied to academia. I actually feared encountering a Democrat judge with an ax to grind against a high-profile conservative. This book became my only means to present my case to the public and let the court of public opinion decide judgment on Gay's unattributed use of my ideas and my verbiage from *Black Faces, Black Interests*.

There's an old saying that paints the picture here: "You can't fight city hall." That's what an individual is up against when seeking justice against a filthy-rich powerhouse such as Harvard University/Harvard Corporation. Harvard's message to me was a finger-wagging scolding to not even try it, and, *We are not going to settle with you*. And to borrow from *A Few Good Men*, "You messed with the wrong Marine!!!!"

Bill Ackman, a Harvard alumnus, hedge fund manager, and abundantly generous donor to the school—he reportedly happens to be worth about $4 billion—was among the few in the greater Harvard community calling for Gay's ouster from the time student protests broke out over the war in Gaza, while Gay apparently did little other than bite her tongue, wring her hands, and eventually mention something about "context." Ackman even called for Gay's exit from the university, period, more than just a demotion.[37]

Someone must have been listening to Ackman's reasonable opinions. Less than a week after Gay stepped down as president, reports surfaced that Ackman's wife, Neri Oxman, a former Massachusetts Institute of Technology (MIT) professor, had been accused of several counts of plagiarism in her 2010 doctorate dissertation. Similar charges for other works of hers cropped up as well. It was bad timing for her, and apparent proof that her husband's remarks had painted a target on her back. Someone went to a lot of trouble digging this up about Oxman, obviously putting a lot more muscle into examining her work than anybody at Harvard had done in 1997 in "vetting" Gay's dissertation. Oxman was having to apologize publicly at the same time she was launching her new design firm.[38]

"You know that you struck a chord when they go after your wife, in this case, my love and partner in life," Ackman posted on X, upi.com reported, adding "Part of what makes her human is that she makes mistakes, owns them, and apologizes when appropriate."[39]

That's a lesson Gay should have learned as well.

CHAPTER 7

Outliers

P LAGIARISM, FAIR USE VIOLATIONS, AND AVERSIONS TO ATTRIBUTION and quote marks seem to be gaining acceptance in the academic community as well as in the media in general. "Hurry up, get your work done, collect your praises and citations, and get ready to be promoted up the chain." Ain't it cool what you can do with DEI, which should have been DOA after the Supreme Court issued its thumbs-down on affirmative action? But it lives on at many places, certainly at Harvard. Once-rigid rules of scholarship and journalism have been tossed out the window and into dumpsters when it comes to policing the work of plagiarists, including the serial ones.

If this doesn't make you angry like it does me, you need to check your pulse.

Here's a two-for-one special in the realm of skating off with other people's work, this time involving media icons. No doubt you have heard of at least one of these Hans Brinkers: Prominent targets of plagiarism accusations in the last decade have been CNN segment host and *Washington Post* writer Fareed Zakaria and multiple best-selling author Malcolm Gladwell (*Outliers, The Tipping Point, Blink*, etc.), also a frequent contributor to the *New Yorker*.

The Gay Affair

Zakaria, as sourced from his website (fareedzakaria.com), is described as a *Washington Post* columnist and best-selling author who hosts his own show on CNN. In 2014 he was accused of having plagiarized, or "reused," without attribution the copyrighted works of other writers/authors at least three dozen times in his books and magazine articles and on his television program. In reporting about this in a September 16, 2014, article published on political.com, reporter Dylan Byers contacted two journalism ethics experts, one from the University of Wisconsin-Madison and the other from the Poynter Institute, to review the plagiarism allegations against Zakaria that were originally reported by Our Bad Media. Upon finishing their respective reviews, both of Byers's pundits tagged the plagiarism label on Zakaria.[40]

One of those two experts consulted by Byers was Robert Drechsel, director of the Center for Journalism Ethics at UW-Madison. In an email to *Politico*, he wrote, "Most of the examples provided and analyzed by the bloggers seem to fall into the realm of what is now being called 'patch writing'—using material generated by someone else, without attribution, but rewritten slightly so one cannot call it verbatim copying. It falls within what I would consider plagiarism. Other examples cited by the bloggers [referring to Our Bad Media's report] do appear to be verbatim."[41]

After learning of the charges of plagiarism against him originally reported by Our Bad Media, Zakaria sent an email to *Politico* denying wrongdoing on his part. "These are all facts, not someone else's writing or opinions or expressions."

Back to Byers: "He also referred to the majority of instances as 'cases in my writing where I have cited a statistic that also appeared somewhere else,' suggesting he had merely repeated readily available information."

Note that two years earlier, in 2012, Zakaria had been suspended by both the *Post* and CNN for one instance of plagiarism, which he described simply as "a mistake." The *Post* and CNN stood up for Zakaria, dismissing the plagiarism allegations that Our Bad Media had originally reported in 2014.[42]

Gladwell, too, has had segments of his published work questioned for how close, in some cases verbatim, his wording has matched verbiage that appeared in earlier works authored by others. Not only has Gladwell reportedly used these allegedly pilfered interview-generated quotes without attribution, but he also presented them in such a way as to make it read like he conducted the interviews. Case in point, identified by Our Bad Media, is the Gladwell-authored article "Creation Myth" published in May 2011 in the *New Yorker*. In the piece, Gladwell, who, granted, is a master storyteller, in this case tells a fascinating story about a young Steve Jobs, the founder of Apple. As the story goes, Jobs in 1979 convinced officials at Xerox Corporation to give him access to their PARC facility. As reported by Our Bad Media, "In one passage, Gladwell quotes Jobs as offering Xerox 100,000 shares of Apple for $1M if the company would 'open its kimono,' or allow him to see their research center."[43]

Once Jobs was inside the research facility to eyeball how Xerox made its secret sauce, as Gladwell wrote, this was where Jobs met Xerox engineer Larry Tesler. At some point, Tesler gave the giddy Jobs a sneak preview of the Alto, Xerox's early version of the first PC. Given this opportunity, Jobs, reportedly, used this sneak peek to cast his own vision for what would become the much-ballyhooed Macintosh computer. In the midst of recounting all this in his *New Yorker* piece, Gladwell inserts the following, as shown in a highlighted segment of the article as published by Our Bad Media. (Pay close attention to the segment where Tesler is quoted):

"Jobs had come with one of his software engineers, Bill Atkinson, and Atkinson moved in as close as he could, his nose almost touching the (Alto) screen. 'Jobs was pacing around the room, acting up the whole time,' Tesler recalled (according to Gladwell). 'He was very excited. Then, when he began seeing the things I could do on-screen, he watched for about a minute and started jumping around the room, shouting, "Why aren't you doing anything with this? This is the greatest thing. This is revolutionary!"'"[44]

Great stuff, right? Not exactly. The Tesler quote is reportedly genuine, but it apparently was not Gladwell who interviewed him to get the quote, even though it reads as such, according to Our Bad Media's reporting. In fact, the Tesler quote, to include its introduction with a very similarly worded reference to Bill Atkinson's up-close-and-personal look at the Alto, originally appeared in author Jeffrey S. Young's book *Steve Jobs: The Journey Is the Reward*, published in 1988. According to Our Bad Media, nowhere in his *New Yorker* article does Gladwell make mention of or attribute Young, although he does cite four other sources used in composing his story.[45]

CHAPTER 8

Farewell to Oversight

THERE WAS A TIME WHEN ALMOST ALL UNIVERSITIES were very strict in dealing with students caught cheating or cutting corners by methods such as plagiarism. Times have unquestionably changed.

Much of academia is no longer willing to police academic integrity. People (i.e., ethics-abiding students, professors, and the like) are being cheated as a consequence, and they have no recourse. That's because copyright law doesn't provide them with an alternative. Copyright laws need to be expanded, to include putting some teeth into protecting the ideas, insights, concepts, and conclusions formulated and expressed by authors/writers. There needs to be a place they can go and get justice when someone crosses the line with their material.

As I explained earlier, my intent to initiate a legal case aimed at Harvard quickly became a dead-end street once I got those April 23 "companion" letters (a one-two gut punch) from Roman and Stein laying out that I didn't have a chance, either from a legal-precedent point of view or a financial one. Plus, I was having to work as hard as my attorneys were while trying to familiarize them with this kind of law, a task that for them entailed reading the work (*ca-ching, ca-ching*, on my dime) to understand where the violations occurred. Plus I was tasked with providing them data for the side-by-side (Appendix A, on pages 62-63) of the most serious instances of Gay's pilferings.

The even harder part was explaining the violations of academic integrity that involved theft of ideas and conclusions instead of the direct lifting of actual sentences and phrases. Finally, the lawyers were ready to approach Harvard expecting that the weight of the evidence from the side-by-side comparisons of Gay's work and mine, as well as the significance of my work, would convince the Harvard lawyers to settle the case. Fat chance! We would soon learn that Harvard's big-dog lawyers eat people like me for breakfast. I would have had better luck trying to rehabilitate Darth Vader and turn him back into Anakin Skywalker. Then came a silver lining. God used Professor Blumstein, a brilliant legal scholar, to put things in perspective and give me the right advice that would steer me away from a battle with a bully that shows no mercy when it comes to those who would challenge its authority and dominion over all things intellectual.

Professor Blumstein painted most clearly the picture of the consequences of a loser-pays provision. He carefully read the letters and the complaint before discussing the legal theory of the case with my attorneys. (You can read my compete legal complaint in Appendix C starting on page 82.) It was Blumstein who caused me to weigh the costs and benefits of going up against Harvard. "Carol," he said, "I care about you, and I don't want to see you hurt in the process of trying to fight Harvard. There is great risk of financial harm to you if you pursue a case against them and lose. What happened to you was wrong. It was clearly a violation of academic integrity that should have been addressed. I am not an expert on copyright law, but what I do know would cause me to advise you and your attorneys to pursue a different legal theory. Copyright law does not protect the theft of ideas; therefore, it would be difficult for you to win your case against Harvard University." Another factor was my inability to raise the minimum of $100,000 needed for a trial that could easily have exceeded $250,000.

Reminding me, in case I had forgotten, Professor Blumstein said a better approach might be for me to write a book about the situation or organize an academic conference about plagiarism in higher education. You might call it *The Gay Affair*, he jokingly said in passing.

Plagiarism is a perennial problem in academia. Publish or perish means that desperate people are always hunting for new ideas. It affects graduate students, and young scholars risk further career harm if they go up against a big-named scholar (such as Gay) that the university wants to protect. Because of the discussion, I mulled it over and talked with people who had been financially supportive of the lawsuit. Dr. Robert Shillman, known as Dr. Bob, was one of these men. Dr. Bob concurred that I needed to release the matter. He confessed that he has sued many people over the years even when he knew it would be difficult to win. "The only reason to sue," he said, "is to make the offending party lose sleep. I can guarantee you, Claudine Gay and Harvard attorneys will not lose any sleep over this matter. In fact, you are the only person likely to suffer." Dr. Bob agreed that I should explore other avenues to draw attention to the matter. At this point, I had more than $30,000 in legal expenses. I was nowhere near raising the money needed to go to trial. I swallowed my pride and ended the legal process against Harvard. I also notified my supporters. Many of them encouraged me to continue. Letting Harvard off the legal hook hurt because it felt like I had backed down. Actually, I used common sense. I would rest and regroup for another day.

When I left the lunch meeting with Professor Blumstein, I knew that he had given me some wise advice. I had to find another way to hold Harvard and their DEI poster child Claudine Gay accountable. So much work and money had gone into the complaint, I decided that I owed it to supporters to make the documents public. Perhaps this can help other people in similar situations. Academia has lost considerable credibility in recent decades because of the progressive indoctrination taking place on many campuses around the nation. Academic standards have taken a backseat to partisan activism.

One of the things I have learned from this experience and how copyright law really works is that the clock starts ticking the moment you become aware of the plagiarism. I found out on December 10, 2023 that Gay had plagiarized me twenty-six years earlier. If I had known about this when it occurred, I might have raised a stink that would have led to some corrections. Going back even a few more years before that, if I had continued being a congressional scholar, I would have read her "brilliant" work and found particular sections of it troublesome.

The harm done to me is complicated. I have certainly had a successful career. For those outside of academia, one's standing in the profession is determined by the number of academic citations of your work that turns up in social science and law databases. If someone steals an idea and fails to credit the author, it sets in motion a ripple effect, in that people who read the pilfered ideas have no way of knowing the original source, and its author misses out on the citation. When work is properly cited, a book or article might contain multiple references to the work that inspired the author's decision to address that particular issue. There are intangible harms that cannot be quantified. As I stated previously, Gay would not have authored that particular dissertation framed in the manner it was, without the influence of *Black Faces, Black Interests*, that was at the center of minority representation in the mid-late 1990s. She has benefitted financially for decades from the work that started with her dissertation. (See my commentary and excerpts from Gay's dissertation abstract and introduction in Appendix D starting on page 98.)

Back in the mid-1990s the world of political science was smitten with the existence of *the* Claudine Gay, the brilliant black political science student at Harvard. Perhaps, when you are labeled as brilliant no one bothers to looks too closely at your work. Me, I was smart and provocative; she was brilliant.

At about the same time she was becoming "the Brilliant Claudine Gay," I was evolving into "the Controversial Carol Swain." Ironically, those nicknames became problematical for both of us. For me, it meant some doors started closing in front of me, as would eventually occur over time, creating the circumstances that led to my early retirement from Vanderbilt University. I have sympathy for the Brilliant Claudine Gay because I believe that she and I were both anomalies for different reasons. Perhaps, no one asked the right questions to properly vet her because there was a need and quest to advance black scholars which were viewed as being in short supply. Harvard had before them a perfectly groomed person to walk amongst the most powerful individuals in the world.

Once Gay was identified in late 2022 as the person to succeed Lawrence Bacow as Harvard president, others, finally, started scrutinizing Gay's record and work prior to her presidential ascent, when earlier it appeared no one had cared enough to sift through her work. "The Brilliant Claudine Gay" had done her undergraduate work at Stanford and Princeton, and her PhD at Harvard. Along the way she won a prize for her senior thesis, and then a prize for her later-to-be-tainted dissertation. What was there to worry about? Certainly, she deserved to be fast-tracked, right?

Looking at it from the outside, I question whether her PhD was earned on the basis of the work presented. As far as I know, she has made no corrections of the five instances of verbatim pilfering of my work, and I am not aware of added sentences to the literature review. While I, a senior citizen who hails from poverty, travel around the country speaking and consulting, Gay has a lifetime appointment at what has been considered the most elite academic institution in the world. Her reportedly near-million-dollar annual salary at Harvard should be enough to cover all of her needs through retirement. Gay could afford a world-class attorney and the indemnification that Harvard would have provided its former president. Through it all, she should not have blamed racial animus for the circumstances that led to her resignation from the presidency of Harvard.

What happened to Gay was that the chickens came home to roost. Harvard University made a momentous decision. The Harvard Corporation and Board of Overseers, the institution's governing bodies, would rather have Gay remain at the institution teaching "Reading and Research" than deal with the politics of removing a black, tenured professor who had been elevated as a symbol of the University's commitment to address historic wrongs. Instead of seeking a black descendant of slaves to be its first black president, the University opted for a descendant of immigrant Blacks as the visible symbol of its racial progress. Their actions backfired. Instead of improving race relations and advancing the cause of racial ethnic minorities in higher education, Harvard's handling of the situation has been a setback for high-achieving racial and ethnic minorities and for the reputation of the once-world-class university. Rather than condemn plagiarism, its leaders opted to redefine and reimagine the violation of a grievous act that pierces the heart of academic excellence.

Justifying and redefining plagiarism is not unique to Harvard; whenever high-profile individuals are caught engaging in plagiarism, it is often downplayed and swept under the rug. We have seen this pattern with historians Doris Kearns Goodwin, Stephen Ambrose, and Kevin Kruse. These scholars have suffered no apparent professional harm for pilfering from other people's works. On the other hand, students caught cheating have suffered more consequences than their teachers. These double standards should not be allowed to continue. If cheating is wrong for students, then it is also wrong for professors, administrators, and researchers. Let's hope that more reasonable minds prevail in higher education. Perhaps, academic integrity can be revived. If that happens, it will have a positive ripple effect across the world, even impacting K-12 educational institutions.

Notes

1. Christopher F. Rufo, "Claudine Gay's Data Problem," *City Journal*, January 4, 2024, https://www.city-journal.org/article/claudine-gays-data-problem, viewed October 30, 2024.

2. Bianca Quilantan, "Harvard Governing Board, Activists Say Former President Was a Victim of Racism," *Politico*, January 2, 2024, https://www.politico.com/news/2024/01/02/harvard-presidents-resignation-fuels-accusations-of-racism-from-black-leaders-00133543, viewed October 30, 2024.

3. Aaron Sibarium, "Harvard President Claudine Gay Hit With Six New Charges of Plagiarism," *Washington Free Beacon*, January 1, 2024, https://freebeacon.com/campus/harvard-president-claudine-gay-hit-with-six-new-charges-of-plagiarism/, viewed October 23, 2024.

4. Sophia Nguyen, "The Plagiarism Allegations Against Ex-Harvard President Claudine Gay, Explained," *Washington Post*, January 4, 2024, https://www.washingtonpost.com/books/2024/01/04/claudine-gay-plagiarism-examples-harvard/, viewed December 2, 2024.

5. Emma H. Haidar and Cam E. Kettles, "Former Harvard Corporation Head William Lee '72 Helped Prepare Gay Ahead of Testimony, Highlighting Complex Dual Roles," *Harvard Crimson*, December 29, 2023, https://www.thecrimson.com/article/2023/12/29/wilmerhale-testimony-prep/, viewed October 18, 2024.

Notes

6. Isabel Vincent, "Elise Stefanik Rips Harvard After School Hired Ex-Board Leader and Professor's Law Firm to Probe Ousted Prez Claudine Gay," *New York Post*, January 26, 2024, https://nypost.com/2024/01/26/news/harvard-hired-law-firm-of-ex-board-leader-to-investigate-claudine-gay/, viewed October 18, 2024.

7. Vincent, "Elise Stefanik Rips Harvard After School Hired Ex-Board Leader and Professor's Law Firm to Probe Ousted Prez Claudine Gay," *New York Post*, January 26, 2024.

8. Denyse O'Leary, "Does Plagiarism Really Matter Anymore," mindmatters.ai, January 13, 2024, https://mindmatters.ai/2024/01/does-plagiarism-really-matter-any-more/, viewed October 15, 2024.

9. Andrew Lawrence, "Harvard's Claudine Gay Was Ousted for 'Plagiarism'. How Serious Was It Really?" *Guardian,* January 6, 2004, www.theguardian.com/education/2024/jan/06/harvard-claudine-gay-plagiarism, viewed October 16, 2024.

10. Yaron Steinbuch, "Harvard Finds More 'Duplicative Language' in President Claudine Gay's Work as Congress Investigates Plagiarism," *New York Post*, December 21, 2023, https://nypost.com/2023/12/21/news/harvard-finds-more-duplicative-language-in-presidents-work/, viewed November 4, 2024.

11. Lawrence, "Harvard's Claudine Gay Was Ousted for 'Plagiarism'. How Serious Was It Really?" *Guardian*, January 6, 2004.

12. Patrick McDonald, "Former Harvard Pres Claudine Gay Receives 'Leadership and Courage' Award Despite Controversy-Plagued Tenure," *Campus Reform*, October 9, 2024, https://www.campusreform.org/article/former-harvard-pres-claudine-gay-receives-leadership-courage-award-despite-controversy-plagued-tenure/26521, viewed October 17, 2024.

13. McDonald, "Former Harvard Pres Claudine Gay Receives 'Leadership and Courage' Award Despite Controversy-Plagued Tenure" *Campus Reform*, October 9, 2024.

14. Carol M. Swain, video commentary on social media, October 17, 2024, https://www.facebook.com/Carolmswain.1/videos/433641086035875.

Notes

15. Christopher Rufo, "Kamala Harris's Plagiarism Problem," christopherrufo.com, October 14, 2024, christopherrufo.com/p/kamala-harriss-plagiarism-problem, viewed October 18, 2024.

16. Rufo, "Kamala Harris's Plagiarism Problem," christopherrufo.com, October 14, 2024.

17. Stephanie Saul, Vimal Patel, and Dylan Freedman, "Conservative Activist Seizes on Passages from Harris Book," *New York Times*, October 14, 2024, https://www.nytimes.com/2024/10/14/us/christopher-rufo-kamala-harris-book.html, viewed October 18, 2024.

18. Ariel Zilber, " NY Times Accused of 'Lying about' Kamala Harris Plagiarism Allegations to Minimize Scandal, *New York Post*, October 15, 2024, news.yahoo.com/news/ny-times-accused-lying-kamala-154856386.html, viewed October 18, 2024.

19. Ariel Zilber, " NY Times Accused of 'Lying about' Kamala Harris Plagiarism Allegations to Minimize Scandal, *New York Post*, October 15, 2024.

20. E. J. Dionne Jr. , "Biden Admits Plagiarism in School but Says It Was Not 'Malevolent,'" *New York Times*, September 18, 1987, https://www.nytimes.com/1987/09/18/us/biden-admits-plagiarism-in-school-but-says-it-was-not-malevolent.html, viewed November 11, 2024.

21. Luke Rosiak, "University of Maryland President Copied Rocket Science Paper from Aussie Student," *Daily Wire*, September 7, 2024, https://www.dailywire.com/news/university-of-maryland-president-copied-rocket-science-paper-from-aussie-student, viewed October 15, 2024.

22. Luke Rosiak, "University of Maryland President Copied Rocket Science Paper from Aussie Student," dailywire.com, September 7, 2024.

23. Christina Morales, "University of South Carolina President Resigns After Speech Blunders," *New York Times*, May 13, 2021, https://www.nytimes.com/2021/05/13/us/usc-president-speech-plagiarism.html, viewed October 16, 2021.

24. Morales, "University of South Carolina President Resigns After Speech Blunders," *New York Times*, May 13, 2021.
25. David K. Li and Evan Bush, "Stanford University President Marc Tessier-Lavigne Resigns After Flaws Were Found in His Research," NBC News, July 19, 2023, https://www.nbcnews.com/news/us-news/stanford-university-president-marc-tessier-lavigne-announces-resignati-rcna95141, viewed October 16, 2024.
26. Li and Bush, "Stanford University President Marc Tessier-Lavigne Resigns After Flaws Were Found in His Research," NBC News, July 19, 2023.
27. Christopher Rufo, "Welcome to My Substack," https://christopherrufo.com/about, viewed September 16, 2024.
28. Anastasia Kaliabakos, "Chris Brunet: Who Is the Man Behind Gay's Ouster at Harvard?", *American Conservative*, January 14, 2024, https://www.theamericanconservative.com/the-man-behind-claudine-gays-ouster/, viewed September 16, 2024.
29. Kaliabakos, "Chris Brunet: Who Is the Man Behind Gay's Ouster at Harvard?", *American Conservative*.
30. Kaliabakos, *American Conservative*.
31. Olivia Land and Alex Oliveira, "Embattled Harvard President Claudine Gay Resigns After Plagiarism, Antisemitism Scandals," *New York Post*, January 2, 2024, nypost.com/2024/01/02/news/embattled-harvard-president-claudine-gay-set-to-resign-after-plagiarism-antisemitism-scandals/, viewed September 28, 2024.
32. Emma H. Haidar and Cam E. Kettles, "The Rise and Fall of Harvard President Claudine Gay," *Harvard Crimson*, January 3, 2024, www.thecrimson.com/article/2024/1/3/claudine-gay-rise-and-fall/, viewed September 28, 2024.
33. Haidar and Kettles, "The Rise and Fall of Harvard President Claudine Gay," *Harvard Crimson*.
34. Christopher Rufo and Christopher Brunet, "Is Claudine Gay a Plagiarist?", cfhristopherrufo.com, December 10, 2023, https://christopher-

rufo.com/p/is-claudine-gay-a-plagiarist/comments, viewed October 19, 2024. Reprinted with permission.

35. Land and Oliveira, "Embattled Harvard President Claudine Gay Resigns After Plagiarism, Antisemitism Scandals," *New York Post*, January 2, 2024, https://nypost.com/2024/01/02/news/embattled-harvard-president-claudine-gay-set-to-resign-after-plagiarism-antisemitism-scandals/, viewed November 17, 2024.

36. Haidar and Kettles, "The Rise and Fall of Harvard President Claudine Gay," *Harvard Crimson*.

37. Ehren Wynder, "Wife of Donor Who Called For Harvard President's Firing Faces Plagiarism Accusations," upi.com, January 6, 2024, https://www.upi.com/Top_News/US/2024/01/06/nerioxman-plagiarism-mit-billackman-harvard/4351704568678/, viewed October 21, 2024.

38. Wynder, "Wife of Donor Who Called for Harvard President's Firing Faces Plagiarism Accusations," upi.com, January 6, 2024.

39. Wynder.

40. Dylan Byers, "The Wrongs of Fareed Zakaria," politico.com, September 16, 2014, https://www.politico.com/blogs/media/2014/09/the-wrongs-of-fareed-zakaria-195579, viewed October 12, 2024.

41. Byers, "The Wrongs of Fareed Zakaria," politico.com.

42. Byers.

43. @blippoblappo & @crushingbort, "Tipping Points? Malcolm Gladwell Could Use a Few," Our Bad Media, December 11, 2014, https://ourbadmedia.wordpress.com/2014/12/11/tipping-points-malcolm-gladwell-could-use-a-few/, viewed October 12, 2024.

44. @blippoblappo & @crushingbort, "Tipping Points? Malcolm Gladwell Could Use a Few," Our Bad Media.

45. @blippoblappo & @crushingbort.

Appendices

Appendix A: Chart 1
Gay and Swain Side-by-Side Comparison

Gay's Title, Page Number	Gay's Text	Swain's Title, Page Number	Swain's Text Used
Gay, Claudine. *Taking Charge: Black Electoral Success and the Redefinition of American Politics*. Dissertation submitted to the Department of Government, Harvard University, 1997, p. 146	Preston (1978) argued that descriptive representation is "not only desirable but necessary for Black Americans," because, in part, it fulfills a host of psychological needs.	Swain, Carol. *Black Faces, Black Interests: The Representation of African Americans in Congress*. Cambridge: Harvard University Press, 1995, p. 217	The presence of black representatives in Congress, regardless of their political party, **fulfills a host of psychological needs** that are no less important for being intangible. One need only attend an annual Black Caucus legislative weekend to see the pride that the hundreds of blacks who attend the affair have in the group of congressional black representatives. Black representatives are celebrities-icons for their group. **Michael Preston writes: "Symbolic representation is not only desirable but necessary for black Americans."**
Gay, *Taking Charge*, p. 2	To date, social scientists have concentrated their analytical efforts on the ambiguous link between minority office-holding and minority public policy agendas, between descriptive representation (the statistical correspondence of demographic characteristics) and substantive representation (the correspondence of legislative goals and priorities) [Gay, p. 2 seeks to counter conclusions from *Black Faces*. Dissertation students have to make a case for the importance of their work. By not citing *Black Faces*, readers would assume these are her original ideas.]	Swain, *Black Faces, Black Interests*, p. 5	Pitkin distinguishes between **"descriptive representation," the statistical correspondence of the demographic characteristics** of representatives with those constituents, and more **"substantive representation," the correspondence between representatives' goals** and those of their constituents.

Appendix A: Chart 2
Gay and Swain Side-by-Side Comparison

Gay's Title, Page Number	Gay's Text	Swain's Title, Page Number	Swain's Text Used
Gay, *Taking Charge*, p. 92	Since the 1950s, the reelection rate for incumbent House members has rarely dipped below 90%. In 1994 it was 92.3% (Swain 1997). [Gay added a comma after "1950s." She also has a citation for the second sentence.]	Swain, *Black Faces, Black Interests*, p. 97	**Since the 1950s, the reelection rate for House members has rarely dipped below 90 percent.** For 1988 and 1990 it was 98.4 and 96.9, respectively. The reelection rate was 82.1 percent in 1992, and 92.3 percent in 1994.
Gay, *Taking Charge*, p. 2	**Gay's dissertation sought to refute Swain's conclusions about black representation.** The existence of white officeholders equally likely to support black policy interests would render black office-holding insignificant. Whether there are, in fact, qualitative differences in the agendas and priorities of black office-holders–with favorable implications for how effectively they serve the interests of black constituents–remains a point of contention. However, that policy consequences are the appropriate subject of inquiry has not been a matter of debate.	Swain, *Black Faces, Black Interests*, p. 211 **See similarities between Gay and Swain's works.**	White representatives who support the goals of blacks, however, these goals are defined, are a further source of black representation. Yet descriptive representation of blacks guarantees only black faces and is, at best, an intangible good; substantive representation can be measured by a politician's performance on indicators such as voting and casework. Many of the white members of Congress perform well or better on the indicators used in this book than some black representatives. [These passages depict ideas expressed in Swain's work that Gay used to frame her ideas.]
Gay, Claudine. *Taking Charge: Black Electoral Success and the Redefinition of American Politics.*	**Gay's dissertation and 2001-2002 articles on representation were framed around conclusions in *Black Faces, Black Interests*.**	Swain, *Black Faces, Black Interests*, p. 212	What difference does the race of the representative make for the representation of black policy preferences?

Appendix B: Letter 1
Kleinman Jan. 3, 2024 Letter to Harvard

COMMON SENSE COUNSEL® LLP
UNCOMMON ATTORNEYS

VIA FedEx

January 3, 2024

The Harvard Corporation
The Fellows of Harvard College
Alan Garber, Interim President
Penny Pritzker, Senior Fellow
Timothy R. Barakett, Treasurer
Kenneth I. Chenault
Mariano-Florentino Cuéllar
Paul J. Finnegan
Biddy Martin
Karen Gordon Mills
Diana L. Nelson
Tracy Pun Palandjian
Shirley M. Tilghman
Theodore V. Wells, Jr.
Harvard University
Massachusetts Hall
Cambridge, MA 02138

Dear Fellows of Harvard College,

We are attorneys for the acclaimed African-American scholar Carol Swain, Ph.D. Dr. Swain is the author of many respected academic works, including the Woodrow Wilson prize-winning *Black Faces, Black Interests: The Representation of African Americans in Congress* (Harvard University Press, 1993, 1995). Dr. Swain's book is recognized

APPENDIX B: SWAIN-HARVARD LEGAL CORRESPONDENCE

as a seminal work on Black representation in Congress and has been cited in two U.S. Supreme Court decisions.

Through recent media reports investigating the academic credentials of former Harvard Corporation President Dr. Claudine Gay, Dr. Swain was made aware that *Black Faces, Black Interests: The Representation of African Americans in Congress* was the subject of plagiarism, use without citation, and unlawful copying.

Black Faces, Black Interests: The Representation of African Americans in Congress is the product of Dr. Swain's original and independent research. Accordingly, Dr. Swain is entitled to certain rights and remedies arising from the prohibited use of its content. Through its acts, omissions, and public statements surrounding the use of Dr. Swain's work, the Harvard Corporation is now invested in this matter and its subsequent outcome. Dr. Swain therefore requires the Harvard Corporation to provide clarification on the following:

- What is "duplicative language," and how do verbatim copying and
duplicative language differ?

- Does the identical replication of another author's language require the use of quotation marks?

- Under what circumstances would the retroactive insertion "of citations and quotation marks that were omitted from the original publications" be permissible in an academic setting?

- Does Dr. Gay's *Taking Charge: Black Electoral Success and the Redefinition of American Politics* satisfy *Harvard University's Guidelines for The PhD Dissertation*, effective July 1, 1997?

- How many instances of duplicative language in a scholarly work would constitute plagiarism?
Would five instances of duplicative language constitute plagiarism? Would 50?

Appendix B: Swain-Harvard Legal Correspondence

- Would the discovery of plagiarism in a dissertation after a Harvard degree has been awarded impact the status or validity of the degree conferred?

Thank you for your courtesy and consideration. We look forward to receiving the Harvard Corporation's response to the foregoing questions no later than January 8, 2024.

Sincerely,

Robert Kleinman

[signature]

cc: Dr. Carol Swain

Author's note: The letters reproduced throughout this Appendix have been reformatted to fit the space allotted in these pages. The letters were commissioned by and authored in collaboration with author Carol Swain.

Appendix B: Letter 2
Lackey Feb. 16, 2024 1st Demand Letter

This "demand" letter was written in response to a Jan. 17 letter written to my then-attorney Robert Kleinman by Harvard Vice President and General Counsel Diane E. Lopez. In answering our Jan. 3 letter to Harvard, Lopez directed us to contact Claudine Gay, who by then had returned to a faculty appointment in Harvard's Faculty of Arts and Sciences. At this point, I had hired the law firm of Lackey McDonald. I assisted Joseph L. Lackey III in drafting the following letter.

February 16th, 2024

TO: Diane E. Lopez
Vice President and General Counsel Massachusetts Hall
11 Harvard Yard
Cambridge, Massachusetts 02138

RE: Dr. Carol Swain v. Dr. Claudine Gay and Harvard Corporation

To whom it may concern,

Our firm represents Dr. Carol Swain in the copyright infringement action against Dr. Claudine Gay and Harvard Corporation (hereinafter "Harvard") in relation to the plagiarism and copyright infringement of Dr. Swain's highly acclaimed work, *Black Faces, Black Interests: The Representation of African Americans in Congress*. We hope to resolve this matter before filing suit, and as such, we put forth the following:

APPENDIX B: SWAIN-HARVARD LEGAL CORRESPONDENCE

It is our assertion that Dr. Gay and Harvard have, through some of the works of Dr. Claudine Gay, infringed on the copyrighted work of Dr. Carol Swain. As you are aware, to establish liability for copyright infringement, Dr. Swain must prove (1) ownership of a valid copyright; and (2) copying of constituent elements of the work that are original. *Feist Publ'ns, Inc. v. Rural Tel. Serv. Co.*, 499

U.S. 340, 361 (1991). Copyright registration presumptively establishes the first prong of copyright infringement. *Lexmark Int'l, Inc. v. Static Control Components, Inc.*, 387 F.3d 522, 534 (6th Cir. 2004). The second prong tests whether any copying occurred and whether the portion of the work copied is entitled to copyright protection. Id.

I. Ownership of a valid copyright.

Dr. Swain's *Black Faces, Black Interests: The Representation of African Americans in Congress* was originally published in 1993 and then expanded in 1995 (hereinafter "Black Faces").

Black Faces won multiple awards and gained international attention and reputation. Among the recognition *Black Faces* received included being named as one of the seven outstanding academic books of 1994 by *Library Choice Journal*, the winner of the 1994 Woodrow Wilson prize (the "best book published in the United States during the prior year on government, politics or international affairs"). At the time, the Woodrow Wilson Prize was the highest professional prize a political scientist could win. *Black Faces* also was the co-winner of the V.O. Key Award and won the 1995 D. B. Hardeman Prize for the best scholarly work on the U.S. Congress during a biennial period. Additionally, the work has been cited by Justice Kennedy in *Johnson V. Degrandy*, 512 U.S. 997, 1027 (1994) and twice by Justice O'Connor in Georgia v. Ashcroft, 539 U.S. (2003).

The 1993 and 1995 versions of *Black Face* are registered in the United States Copyright Office. The copyright number of the 1993 version is TX0003551319 and the 1995 expanded version is TX0004132156. Dr. Swain's *Black Faces* constitutes an original work of authorship as set forth in 17 U.S.C.S. § 102(a)(1), and the registration of each work presumptively establishes a validly copyrighted work. Accordingly, Dr. Carol Swain's work *Black Faces* is entitled to full statutory and common law copyright protections.

II. Infringement.

Copyright infringement occurs when an individual copies the original elements of the copyrighted work.

Originality exists as a standard for infringement, though not as a stringent one. Feist, 499 U.S. at 362. Copyright laws protect the elements of a work that possess more than a de minimis quantum of creativity. Id. at 363. Direct infringement of a copyrighted work arises from the violation of any one of the exclusive rights of a copyright owner. *Bridgeport v. Rhyme Syndicate Music*, 376 F.3d 615, 621 (6th Circ. 1994). When two or more parties contribute to the infringement on a copyright, they are held jointly and severally liable for the damages incurred by the copyright owner. *Corbis Corp. v. Starr*, No. 3:07CV3741, 2009 U.S. Dist. LEXIS 79626, 2009 WL 2901308, at *4 (N.D. Ohio Sept. 2, 2009).

In addition to joint and several liability, a party may also be held vicariously liable for copyright infringement. Vicarious liability for copyright infringement is established if the defendant received a financial benefit from the direct infringement and had the right and ability to stop or limited the infringement but failed to do so. *Metro-Goldwyn-Mayer Studios Inc. v. Grokster, Ltd.*, 545 U.S. 913, 930, (2005).

Dr. Swain is the holder of the copyright in *Black Faces* and all the original elements contained therein. *Black Faces* contains Dr. Swain's original ideas regarding African American congressional representation. Dr. Gay takes those original and protected ideas of Dr. Swain, as printed in her work, and poses it as her own throughout her dissertation and other works.[1] Dr. Gay argues the other side of Dr. Swain's position, but

---

[1] Gay, Claudine, *The Effect of Black Congressional Representation on Political Participation*, Volume 95, No. 3, *American Political Science Review*, 589-602, Sep. 2001); Gay, Claudine, *The Effect of Minority Districts and Minority Representation*

APPENDIX B: SWAIN-HARVARD LEGAL CORRESPONDENCE

the underlying concepts and ideas that Dr. Gay poses and engages with, are the original works of authorship of Dr. Swain that is contained in *Black Faces*. Specifically, Dr. Gay's dissertation [2] and subsequent works on congressional representation of African Americans have patently infringed on the original work of Dr. Carol Swain without due accreditation or request for the use of these ideas. The cornerstone question that both Dr. Gay and Dr. Swain pose throughout their works is the question of whether African Americans can be appropriately represented at the congressional level by another race, specifically white Americans. Dr. Gay uses the exact same definition, of Substantive Representation [3] and Descriptive Representation, [4] elucidates and draws the basis of her work from that same question.

Harvard directly contributed to the infringement of Dr. Swain's copyright by publishing Dr. Gay's dissertation. Harvard profited from Dr. Gay's infringement in the form of grants and notoriety generated by Dr. Gay's infringed works. Additionally, Harvard owned and published these works and still allows for this material to be distributed and published via numerous outlets. Harvard had the right and ability to stop or limit the infringement but failed to do so. Harvard held a unique position to prevent Dr. Gay from publishing the infringing work yet decided to willfully allow the infringing work to be published or recklessly neglected to properly review the work for plagiarism and copyright infringement. Independent analyses from the *Harvard*

---

on Political Participation in California, Public Policy Institute of California, (June 2001); Gay, Claudine, *Spirals of Trust? The Effect of Descriptive Representation on the Relationship between Citizens and Their Government,* Volume 46, No. 4, American Political Science Review, 717-732, (Oct. 2022).

[2] Gay, Claudine, *Replication data for: Taking Charge: Black Electoral Success and the Redefinition of American Politics,* Harvard Dataverse, V3 (1997) (republished in 2008).

[3] Gay, Claudine: "substantive representation (the correspondence of legislative goals and priorities)"; Swain, Carol: "substantive representation,' the correspondence between representatives' goals and those of their constituents."

[4] Gay, Claudine: "descriptive representation (the statistical correspondence of demographic characteristics)"; Swain, Carol: "descriptive representation,' the statistical correspondence of the demographic characteristics."

Appendix B: Swain-Harvard Legal Correspondence

Crimson and CNN state instances of plagiarism by Dr. Gay violated the university's policies, despite Harvard stating otherwise.

Dr. Gay infringed on Dr. Swain's copyrighted works, and Harvard contributed to and furthered Dr. Gay's infringement.

III. Damages.

Dr. Swain may recover either actual damages or statutory damages as a remedy for copyright infringement.

Actual damages include damages suffered by the Plaintiff, such as lost profits, and any additional profits of the infringer as a result of the infringement. 17 U.S.C. § 504(b). Courts have the discretion to grant statutory damages in the amount of $750.00 to $30,000.00 per infringement. 17

U.S.C. § 504(c)(1). However, if the infringement was willful, the courts may increase the statutory damages to $150,000.00 per infringement. 17 U.S.C. § 504(c)(2). A party willfully infringes upon the plaintiff's copyright if it knowingly to recklessly copies another's work. *Zomba Enters., Inc. v. Panorama Records, Inc.*, 491 F.3d 574, 585 (6th Cir. 2007). The courts also have discretion to award the recovery of full costs and reasonable attorney's fee to the prevailing party. 17 U.S.C. § 505.

Here, Dr. Gay clearly engaged in willful infringement of Dr. Swain's protected works. Dr. Gay engaged in numerous acts of plagiarism throughout her career, further displaying her willful nature in stealing from the protected works of others.[5] At the time of Dr. Gay's infringement, *Black Faces* was an internationally recognized and award-winning work in the political science field. Dr. Gay has engaged in verbatim copying of *Black Faces* (and the copyrighted works of others) in numerous published articles. Additionally, Dr. Gay utilized Dr. Swain's original ideas concerning African American congressional representation as the central idea in which she structures her dissertation, and numerous subsequent works. Dr. Gay fails to properly attribute the original work of Dr. Swain throughout all her works despite routinely engaging in review and discussion on the works.

---

[5] https://freebeacon.com/wp-content/uploads/2024/01/Complaint2.pdf

Appendix B: Swain-Harvard Legal Correspondence

IV. Compromise and Settlement.

At this juncture Dr. Carol Swain is willing to the following terms for an Offer of Compromise and Settlement:

a. A retraction or correction to the works of Dr. Claudine Gay. Dr. Carol Swain would demand, at a minimum, a formal correction to the works of Dr. Claudine Gay. Specifically, Dr. Swain demands Harvard make a formal correction to Dr. Gay's dissertation and subsequent works by citing Dr. Carol Swain's work *Black Faces* in her work; and

b. A monetary settlement in the amount of Six Million Dollars ($6,000,000.00). It has come to our attention that the Dr. Claudine Gay's Dissertation, has 1,346 downloads to date on Harvard Dataverse's website. This set of infringements alone constitutes damages in the tens of millions of dollars, even if the infringement is not deemed to be willful, which we deem unlikely considering Harvard's posture in the academic community and the acclaim that Dr. Swain's work had received just a few years prior.

c. If these terms can be met, Dr. Carol Swain, is willing to execute a Release of Claims to put this behind her and the Harvard Corporation.

We await your response and hope we can arrive at a fair and reasonable resolution to this issue.

THIS LETTER IS BEING SENT FOR PURPOSES OF COMPROMISE AND SETTLEMENT ONLY.

Kindest Regards,

Joseph L. Lackey, III., Esq. jlackey3@lackeypllc.com

Author's note: The letters reproduced throughout this Appendix have been reformatted to fit the space allotted in these pages. The letters were commissioned by author Carol Swain.

Appendix B: Letter 3
Lackey Apr. 5, 2024, 2nd Demand Letter

April 5th, 2024

TO: Neil K. Roman, Esq.
Covington & Burling LLP
One City Center
850 Tenth Street, NW
Washington, DC 20001
nroman@cov.com

Alison Stein, Esq.
Jenner & Block
1155 Avenue of the Americas
New York, New York 10036
astein@jenner.com

RE: Dr. Carol Swain v. Dr. Claudine Gay and Harvard Corporation

All,

As you are aware, our firm represents Dr. Carol Swain in the copyright infringement action against Dr. Claudine Gay and Harvard Corporation (hereinafter "Harvard") in relation to the plagiarism and copyright infringement of Dr. Swain's highly acclaimed work, *Black Faces, Black Interests: The Representation of African Americans in Congress*.

Appendix B: Swain-Harvard Legal Correspondence

It is our assertion that Dr. Gay and Harvard have, through some of the works of Dr. Claudine Gay, infringed on the copyrighted work of Dr. Carol Swain.

Dr. Swain's *Black Faces, Black Interests: The Representation of African Americans in Congress* was originally published in 1993 and then expanded in 1995 (hereinafter "*Black Faces*"). *Black Faces* won multiple awards and gained international attention and reputation. Among the recognition *Black Faces* received included being named as one of the seven outstanding academic books of 1994 by *Library Choice Journal*, the winner of the 1994 Woodrow Wilson prize (the "best book published in the United States during the prior year on government, politics or international affairs"). At the time, the Woodrow Wilson Prize was the highest professional prize a political scientist could win. *Black Faces* also was the co-winner of the V.O. Key Award and won the 1995 D. B. Hardeman Prize for the best scholarly work on the U.S. Congress during a biennial period. Additionally, the work has been cited by Justice Kennedy in *Johnson V. Degrandy*, 512 U.S. 997, 1027 (1994) and twice by Justice O'Connor in *Georgia v. Ashcroft*, 539 U.S. (2003).

The 1993 and 1995 versions of *Black Faces* are registered in the United States Copyright Office. The copyright number of the 1993 version is TX0003551319 and the 1995 expanded version is TX0004132156. Dr. Swain's *Black Faces* constitutes an original work of authorship as set forth in 17 U.S.C.S. § 102(a)(1), and the registration of each work presumptively establishes a validly copyrighted work. Accordingly, Dr. Carol Swain's work *Black Faces* is entitled to full statutory and common law copyright protections.

Dr. Swain is the holder of the copyright in *Black Faces* and all the original elements contained therein. *Black Faces* contains Dr. Swain's original ideas regarding African American congressional representation. Dr. Gay takes those original and protected ideas of Dr. Swain, as printed in her work, and poses it as her own throughout her dissertation and other works.[1] Dr. Gay argues the other side

---

[1] Gay, Claudine, *The Effect of Black Congressional Representation on Political Participation*,

APPENDIX B: SWAIN-HARVARD LEGAL CORRESPONDENCE

of Dr. Swain's position, but the underlying concepts and ideas that Dr. Gay poses and engages with, are the original works of authorship of Dr. Swain that is contained in *Black Faces*. Specifically, Dr. Gay's dissertation [2] and subsequent works on congressional representation of African Americans have patently infringed on the original work of Dr. Carol Swain without due accreditation or request for the use of these ideas. The cornerstone question that both Dr. Gay and Dr. Swain pose throughout their works is the question of whether African Americans can be appropriately represented at the congressional level by another race, specifically white Americans. Dr. Gay uses the exact same definition, of Substantive Representation[3] and Descriptive Representation,[4] elucidates and draws the basis of her work from that same question.

Harvard directly contributed to the infringement of Dr. Swain's copyright by publishing Dr. Gay's dissertation. Harvard profited from Dr. Gay's infringement in the form of grants and notoriety generated by Dr. Gay's infringed works. Additionally, Harvard owned and published these works and still allows for this material to be distributed and published via numerous outlets. Harvard had the right and ability to stop or limit the infringement but failed to do so. Harvard held a unique position to prevent Dr. Gay from publishing the infringing work yet decided to willfully allow the infringing work to be published or recklessly neglected to properly review the work for plagiarism and copyright infringement. Independent analyses from the *Harvard Crimson* and CNN

Volume 95, No. 3, *American Political Science Review*, 589-602, Sep. 2001); Gay, Claudine, *The Effect of Minority Districts and Minority Representation on Political Participation in California*, Public Policy Institute of California, (June 2001); Gay, Claudine, *Spirals of Trust? The Effect of Descriptive Representation on the Relationship between Citizens and Their Government*, Volume 46, No. 4, *American Political Science Review*, 717-732, (Oct. 2022).

[2] Gay, Claudine, *Replication data for: Taking Charge: Black Electoral Success and the Redefinition of American Politics*, Harvard Dataverse, V3 (1997) (republished in 2008).

[3] Gay, Claudine: "substantive representation (the correspondence of legislative goals and priorities)"; Swain, Carol: "'substantive representation,' the correspondence between representatives' goals and those of their constituents."

[4] Gay, Claudine: "descriptive representation (the statistical correspondence of demographic characteristics)"; Swain, Carol: "'descriptive representation,' the statistical correspondence of the demographic characteristics".

Appendix B: Swain-Harvard Legal Correspondence

state instances of plagiarism by Dr. Gay violated the university's policies, despite Harvard stating otherwise.

Dr. Gay infringed on Dr. Swain's copyrighted works, and Harvard contributed to and furthered Dr. Gay's infringement. Dr. Gay clearly engaged in willful infringement of Dr. Swain's protected works. Dr. Gay engaged in numerous acts of plagiarism throughout her career, further displaying her willful nature in stealing from the protected works of others.[5] At the time of Dr. Gay's infringement, *Black Faces* was an internationally recognized and award-winning work in the political science field. Dr. Gay has engaged in verbatim copying of *Black Faces* (and the copyrighted works of others) in numerous published articles. Additionally, Dr. Gay utilized Dr. Swain's original ideas concerning African American congressional representation as the central idea in which she structured her dissertation and numerous subsequent works. Dr. Gay fails to properly attribute the original work of Dr. Swain throughout all her works despite routinely engaging in review and discussion on the works.

In response to Mr. (Neil) Roman's March 5, 2024 Letter, please see Exhibit A to this letter, which represents the list of the copyrighted works of Dr. Swain and instances in which Dr. Gay has copied protectable expression from those works. As we feel, you will see that there is a systematic and overarching pattern of theft of intellectual property and ideas of Dr. Swain's works by Dr. Claudine Gay and, in turn, the Harvard Corporation. It is our position that the list of infringements listed below are certain enumerated instances of infringement, but additionally, it is our contention that Dr. Gay has infringed on the overall work and theories of Dr. Carol Swain.

Please note, that the accompanying Exhibit is not a conclusive and comprehensive list of duplicative and infringing language and that it may be supplemented throughout this process.

---

[5] https://freebeacon.com/wp-content/uploads/2024/01/Complaint2.pdf

Appendix B: Swain-Harvard Legal Correspondence

THIS LETTER IS BEING SENT FOR PURPOSES OF COMPROMISE AND SETTLEMENT ONLY.

Kindest Regards,

/s/ Joseph L. Lackey, III.

Joseph L. Lackey, III., Esq

jlackey3@lackeypllc.com

Author's note: The letters reproduced throughout this Appendix have been reformatted to fit the space allotted in these pages. This letter was commissioned by author Carol Swain. Also, the Exhibit A referred to in this letter contains an error and is not republished here. Instead you are directed to Appendix A in this book for a side-by-side comparison of Gay and Swain.

Appendix B: Letter 4
Summary of Roman's Apr. 23, 2024, Letter

Letter from Neil Roman, Claudine Gay's attorney

On April 23, 2024, we received the long-awaited response from Mr. Roman. After acknowledging the five instances we flagged, and which are seen in Appendix A, Roman argued that there was no infringement of *Black Faces, Black Interests*' copyright:

> Based on the allegations in your letters, including as set forth in your Exhibit A, there is no basis to assert that Dr. Gay has infringed any rights held by Dr. Swain . . . As you are surely aware, it is well settled that concepts and ideas are not protectible expression under the Copyright Act. See 17 U.S.C. § 102(b) ("In no case does copyright protection . . . extend to any idea, procedure, process, system, method of operation, concept, principle, or discovery . . ."); *Mazer v. Stein*, 347 U.S. 201, 217 (1954) ("[A] copyright gives no exclusive right to the art disclosed; protection is given only to the expression of the idea—not the idea itself."). Although copyright law protects "an author's original expression," it does "not give the author the exclusive right to use the ideas expressed in that work." *RJ Control Consultants, Inc. v. Multiject, LLC*, 981 F.3d 446, 455 (6th Cir. 2020).

Roman asserted, "Thus, even though Dr. Gay does not rely on Dr. Swain's 'concepts and ideas' in her dissertation, copyright law affords no protection to Dr. Swain for such 'concepts and ideas.' Put another way, there can be no cognizable copyright claim based on Dr. Swain's 'original ideas' and 'overall work and theories.'"

Elsewhere in the letter, Roman stated, "Your allegation that Dr. Gay's dissertation 'copied' a total of approximately three sentences of material from *Black Faces, Black Interests*, even if true, amounts to *de minimis* use and as such is not actionable. . . . "Setting aside any non-actionable *de minimis* similarities, the alleged passages at issue also do not give rise to a cognizable claim of infringement because 'no reasonable trier of fact could conclude that they are "substantially similar." . . . Dr. Gay's work not only endorses the opposite position as Dr.

Appendix B: Swain-Harvard Legal Correspondence

Swain's, but it also relies upon different research methods, models, and data to reach that position... Put another way, there can be no cognizable copyright claim based on Dr. Swain's 'original ideas' and 'overall work and theories.'"

> Roman's parting shot contained a critically important warning:
>
> *Should you, notwithstanding the above, continue to pursue this frivolous copyright infringement claim against Dr. Gay, we will pursue all legal remedies, including collection of attorney's fees* (talics are mine). Under 17 U.S.C. § 505, a court "may... award a reasonable attorney's fee to the prevailing party[.]" *Bridgeport Music v. Diamond Time*, 371 F.3d 883, 893 n.7 (6th Cir.2004).

Appendix B: Letter 5
Summary of Stein's Apr. 23, 2024, Letter

Letter from Allison Stein, attorney for President and Fellows of Harvard College (the "University") in this matter

Allison Stein's letter arrived on the same day as the one from Neil Roman. Allison Stein is an entertainment and intellectual attorney that Harvard hired to defend the university. It was a double whammy and a piling on designed to bully me into submission. I guess it worked because after six weeks or so of mulling it over and seeking expert advice, I walked away from pursuing a copyright infringement claim, but I did not walk away from the stink of the injustice and my desire to use what happened to me to help others.

Stein referred us to Roman's letter and made these additional points: "Among other things, your Letters make patently clear that you are principally seeking to assert a copyright claim based on unprotectable 'ideas,' rather than protectable expression.... Any alleged copying is *de minimis*, you would be unable to otherwise show substantial similarities between the works at issue, and, if there are any similarities that would meet the standard for copyright infringement, they would nevertheless constitute fair use." It was pointed out that my attorneys had not raised "an actionable infringement claim against the University" and it defended the university with the argument that the "University does not own the copyright to Dr. Gay's dissertation" and that it was not publicly available on Harvard Dataverse website. Instead, it was available through ProQuest, which is not associated with the University.

Lastly, Stein grabbed the bull by the horns and stated: "... you appear to attempt to assert contributory and vicarious liability theories against the University.... Contributory infringement requires a showing that the defendant, 'with knowledge of the infringing activity.' ...[The letter continued], 'vicarious liability requires a showing that a defendant "enjoy[ed] a direct financial benefit from the infringing activity and ha[d] the right and ability to supervise the infringing activity.'" Stein concluded that my attorneys had not met the requirements to show that Harvard was indirectly guilty of failing to police Gay's work or that any University grant Gay received "was based on draft dissertation language or of anything indicating the alleged infringing content had any impact on a grant."

Stein concludes the letter with a repeat of the Neil Roman warning about the folly of me pursuing my claim against Gay. "*Dr. Gay, in light of the infirmities with your claims, the University is prepared to seek reasonable attorneys' fees pursuant to 17 U.S.C. § 505 in the event it is forced to incur the further expense of defending against these frivolous claims.*" (Italics are mine).

A frivolous lawsuit for seeking justice? Call me nuts, but I was willing to pursue what Roman and Stein saw as a weak case, but what my attorneys characterized as the perfect test case to expand copyright law. When my emotions calmed and common sense reasserted herself in the form of wisdom, I decided that the risks of financial ruin that would have long-term implications for my children and grandchildren was not worth the cost of going up against a 500-pound gorilla that could ruin me financially and cause additional stress. I took the high road and wrote this book instead.

Appendix C
My Legal Complaint

The following is the complete complaint against Harvard that I put together with my attorneys and which I was prepared to file to initiate legal action against Harvard while seeking a remedy from them for what I believed, and still believe, harmed me and my work in a professional sense. I decided not to file it after I determined that the financial cost, especially if I lost, would overburden me tremendously, well beyond what I could reasonably afford. I present it here as a resource so you can see how I laid out my whole case. You will note that there are three "Exhibits" that are referenced in this complaint, but I have not included them here because I felt they would not add anything significant to the core narrative of this book.

UNITED STATES DISTRICT COURT
FOR THE MIDDLE DISTRICT OF
TENNESSEE

------------------------------X
DR. CAROL SWAIN,   :   [__Civ. ____(___)(___)]
        Plaintiff,   :
    vs.   :   **COMPLAINT**
DR. CLAUDINE GAY, and   :   [JURY TRIAL DEMANDED]
HARVARD CORP.
        Defendants.   :
------------------------------X

    Plaintiff, Dr. Carol Swain ("Plaintiff"), by and through the undersigned attorneys, for her Complaint against Defendant Dr. Claudine Gay ("Dr. Gay") and Defendant Harvard Corp. ("Harvard"), a Massachusetts corporation (collectively, "Defendants"), alleges, on knowledge as to her own actions, and otherwise on information and belief, as follows:

Appendix C: My Legal Complaint

PRELIMINARY STATEMENT

1. Plaintiff brings this action seeking injunctive and monetary relief for Defendant's intentional infringement of Plaintiff's copyright in Plaintiff's *Black Faces, Black Interests: The Representation of African Americans in Congress* (the "Copyrighted Work" or "Work"). [1]

2. Plaintiff's dissertation was under contract with Harvard University Press in 1989 and was published by Harvard University Press in 1993.

3. Plaintiff's Copyrighted Work expands on a 1989 National Science Foundation-funded dissertation (directed by William R. Keech) titled "The Politics of Black Congressional Representation in the United States" (copyright, University of North Carolina at Chapel Hill).

4. Plaintiff is an award-winning political scientist, published author, and renowned legal scholar in the subject matter area of political science.

5. Plaintiff is a retired American political scientist and legal scholar who was early tenured at Princeton University in 1994 and promoted to full professorship at Vanderbilt University in 1999. Plaintiff retired from Vanderbilt University in 2017. She is a frequent political commentator and has edited or authored twelve books and numerous book chapters, articles, and opinion pieces. She has also appeared in eleven documentary films as an expert. Her interests include education, race relations, immigration, representation, religious liberty, and civil rights law.

6. Plaintiff's Copyrighted Work won the 1994 Woodrow Wilson Prize (award given to the best book published in the United States on government, politics, or international affairs), won the 1995 D. B.

---

[1] Plaintiff authored *Black Faces, Black Interests: The Representation of African Americans in Congress* in 1993. In 1995, Plaintiff authored an expanded version of *Black Faces, Black Interests: The Representation of African Americans in Congress*. "Copyrighted Work" or "Copyrighted Works" shall include both the 1993 and 1995 versions.

Hardeman Prize (the best scholarly work on the U.S. Congress during a biennial period), co-winner of the V. O. Key award, and has been cited by the United States Supreme Court in *Johnson v. Degrandy*, 512 U.S. 997, 1027 (1994) and *Georgia v. Ashcroft*, 539 U.S. 461, 482 (2003). The Copyrighted Work was selected by the Library Choice Journal as one of seven outstanding academic books in 1994. Additionally, Plaintiff's book received praise and criticisms. Lee Daniels, *Washington Post Book World* (1993), "Swain commendable book raises fundamental questions. . . This is impressive work. *American Political Science Review* stated: "An important analysis in an area of growing scholarly debate and controversy."

Georgia Historical Quarterly (1993), "Some will label Swain an apostate for arguing that the policy agenda of Black Americans may be advanced by having fewer, not more majority African-American districts." *Constitutional Commentary* (1994–95), "Unlike many other contributions in the debate, the Swain book is richly empirical. Besides multiple-regression analyses, Professor Swain presents the results of several years of patient interviews with black and white members of Congress and their staffs."

7. In 1993, with an enlarged version published in 1995, Plaintiff created the Copyrighted Work. As a result, Plaintiff is the owner of all copyright rights in the Copyrighted Work. Since creation of the Copyrighted Work, Plaintiff has manufactured, published, distributed, and/or sold copies of the Copyrighted Work in the United States by and through Harvard University Press in 1995, and University Press of America in 2006. The initial copyright from 1993 was obtained by Harvard University, and then as of May 13, 2003, reverted back to Dr. Carol Swain. On or around September 7, 2004, Dr. Carol Swain granted the exclusive right to print, publish, and sell her Work in book form. A copyright was issued in her name for the Work and is registered.

8. Plaintiff owns a federal registration for the Copyrighted Work. The federal registration was originally held by Harvard University,

Appendix C: My Legal Complaint

President, and Fellows of Harvard College. Harvard University, President, and Fellows of Harvard College obtained the original copyright on the 11th day of May 1993 (Copyright Registration Number: TX0003551319) and obtained the copyright for the extended version of the Work on the 25th day of September 1995 (Copyright Registration Number: TX0004132156). All rights reverted back to the Plaintiff as of May 2003.

9. University Press of America obtained a subsequent copyright on the 16th day of August 2006 (Copyright Registration Number: TX0006415820).

10. Plaintiff has sold 6,000 copies of the Copyrighted Work, and the Copyrighted Work remains in print after thirty years and continues to produce sales.

11. The Copyrighted Work remains publicly available via numerous means, including but not limited to Amazon, the Smithsonian Institute, Barnes and Noble, Books-A-Million, and other vendors.

12. All of the claims asserted herein arise out of and are based on Defendant's copying, reproduction, and distribution of Dr. Gay's *Taking Charge: Black Electoral Success and the Redefinition of American Politics*, Harvard Dataverse, V3 (1997) (republished in 2008), and its derivative works: *The Effect of Black Congressional Representation on Political Participation*, Volume 95, No. 3, *American Political Science Review*, 589–602 Sep. 2001; *The Effect of Minority Districts and Minority Representation on Political Participation in California*, Public Policy Institute of California, (June 2001); *Spirals of Trust? The Effect of Descriptive Representation on the Relationship between Citizens and Their Government*, Volume 46, No. 4, *American Political Science Review*, 717–732, (Oct. 2022), (collectively, the "Infringing Works") that are copied from Plaintiff's Copyrighted Work. Plaintiff sues for copyright infringement under the United States Copyright Act of 1976, as amended (the "Copyright Act"), 17 U.S.C. § 101 et seq.

13. Plaintiff seeks all remedies afforded by the Copyright Act, including permanent injunctive relief, Plaintiff's damages and Defendant's

profits from Defendant's willfully infringing conduct, and other monetary relief.

JURISDICTION AND VENUE

14. This Court has jurisdiction over this copyright infringement action pursuant to 28 U.S.C. §§ 1331, 1332(a), and 1338(a).

15. Venue is proper in this district under 28 U.S.C. § 1391(b)(2), because a substantial part of the events or omissions giving rise to the claim occurred in this district.

PARTIES

16. Plaintiff, Dr. Carol Swain, is an individual who resides in Nashville, Tennessee.

Plaintiff is a citizen of Tennessee. Plaintiff is an American political scientist, legal scholar, and a retired professor of political science and law at Vanderbilt University, in Nashville, Tennessee. She has published numerous books on the intersection of race and political representation.

17. On information and belief, Defendant Dr. Claudine Gay, is an individual who resides in Boston, Massachusetts. On information and belief, Defendant is a citizen of Massachusetts. On information and belief, Defendant is an American political scientist and academic administrator who is Wilbur A. Cowett Professor of Government and of African American Studies at Harvard. Defendant Dr. Gay served as the President of Harvard University from July 1, 2023 to January 2, 2024.

18. On information and belief, Defendant Harvard Corp. is a corporation that is incorporated in the state of Massachusetts and has its principal place of business in Braintree, Massachusetts. On information and belief, Defendant Harvard Corp. is the legal entity of Harvard University. Harvard University is a private Ivy League research university in Cambridge, Massachusetts.

APPENDIX C: MY LEGAL COMPLAINT

FACTS

A. <u>Plaintiff and Her Copyrighted Work</u>

19. Plaintiff authored the Copyrighted Work in 1993 and subsequently authored the expanded version in 1995. As a result, Plaintiff owns any and all copyright rights in the Copyrighted Work. A true and correct copy of the Copyrighted Work is attached hereto as Exhibit 1 (not included here).

20. The Copyrighted Work is wholly original, and Plaintiff is the exclusive owner of all right, title, and interest, including all rights under copyright, in the Copyrighted Work.

21. Plaintiff is the owner of valid and subsisting United States Copyright Registration No. TX0003551319 and No. TX0004132156 for the Copyrighted Works, issued by the United States Copyright Office in 1993 then republished in 1995. University Press of America obtained a subsequent copyright in 2006 in the Plaintiff's name, Registration No. TX0006415820. Attached as Exhibit 2 (not included here) are true and correct copies of the registration certificates for Plaintiff's Registration No. TX0003551319, No. TX0004132156, and No. TX0006415820.

22. All rights contained within Registration No. TX0003551319 and No. TX0004132156 reverted back to the Plaintiff on or around May 2003. Attached as Exhibit 3 is a true and correct copy of the Reversion Agreement, reverting the rights in the Copyrighted Work to the Plaintiff.

23. Plaintiff has published and distributed the Copyrighted Work by widespread publication and dissemination, including the Harvard University Press and the University Press of America. This publication has been a tremendous success as the Copyrighted Work received national recognition as one of seven outstanding of 1994 by *Library Choice Journal*, won the 1994 Woodrow Wilson prize, won the 1995 D.B. Hardeman biennial Award, and has been cited by the United States Supreme Court in *Johnson v. Degrandy*, 512 U.S. 997, 1027 (1994) and *Georgia v. Ashcroft*, 539 U.S. 461, 482 (2003).

Appendix C: My Legal Complaint

24. The Copyrighted Work is of significant value to Plaintiff because Plaintiff received national and world-wide acclaim and accreditation for the Copyrighted Work. To this date, Plaintiff sells copies of the Copyrighted Work, and accepts public speaking roles to discuss the copyrighted material contained within the Copyrighted Work. Plaintiff has profited financially from the legal dissemination of this Work and relies on the income associated therewith.

25. The Copyrighted Work was an original contribution to the study of black congressional representation in the U.S. Congress. Plaintiff was the first scholar to conduct a systematic study that applied Dr. Hanna Pitkin's theories from *The Concept of Representation* (1967) to different forms of black representation.

26. Dr. Carol Swain received early tenure at Princeton University as a result of her seminal work in the area of black congressional representation. Her dissertation and furtherance of her work on black congressional representation received funding from the National Science Foundation.

27. The Plaintiff's original expression contained within the Copyrighted Work included applying Hanna Pitkin's *The Concept of Representation* (1967) to the study of black congressional representation.

28. The Plaintiff collected original data at the district level, examined the representational styles of white and black members of Congress, and concluded that there was a tradeoff between black descriptive representation and black substantive representation.

29. In the Copyrighted Work, the Plaintiff expresses that it is possible to have more black representatives in Congress (*Black Faces*) and less black substantive representation (more people to support black interests). Plaintiff's study concluded that whites could represent Blacks and Blacks could represent whites and that voting rights strategies that focused on creating "safe black districts" had the unintended consequence of electing more Republicans.

Appendix C: My Legal Complaint

B. Defendant's Infringing Conduct

30. On information and belief, Defendant Dr. Claudine Gay is a published author and scholar in the subject matter area of political science, a professor at Harvard University, and the former President of Harvard University.

31. Upon information and belief, Defendant Harvard Corp. is a for profit business that includes Harvard University. Defendant Harvard Corp. employs Dr. Claudine Gay and receives millions of dollars in scholarship and grant money used to further the academic prestige of Harvard.

32. Defendant Dr. Gay authored, published, printed, and/or distributed, or caused to be published, printed, and/or distributed *Taking Charge: Black Electoral Success and the Redefinition of American Politics*, Harvard Dataverse, V3 (1997) (republished in 2008); *The Effect of Black Congressional Representation on Political Participation*, Volume 95, No. 3, *American Political Science Review*, 589–602 Sep. 2001; *The Effect of Minority Districts and Minority Representation on Political Participation in California*, Public Policy Institute of California, (June 2001); Spirals of Trust? *The Effect of Descriptive Representation on the Relationship between Citizens and Their Government*, Volume 46, No. 4, *American Political Science Review*, 717–732, (Oct. 2022), which contain virtually identical and/or blatant copying of protectable expressions contained within the Copyrighted Work.

33. On information and belief, the Infringing Work *Taking Charge: Black Electoral Success and the Redefinition of American Politics* ("Taking Charge") has been distributed and/or sold via Harvard's database 1,346 times. On information and belief, Harvard still allows consumers to download *Taking Charge*. Attached hereto as Exhibit 4 (not attached here) is a copy of the Infringing Work, *Taking Charge*.

34. On information and belief, Defendant Dr. Gay obtained physical possession of or otherwise viewed Plaintiff's Copyrighted Work, and intentionally copied the Copyrighted Work to create the Infringing Works. That Defendant Dr. Gay copied the Copyrighted Work when

she created the Infringing Works is evidenced by the striking similarities between the Copyrighted Work and the Infringing Works, which cannot possibly be explained other than as a result of copying, failure to attribute proper citation to the striking similarities, and Defendant Dr. Gay's access to the Copyrighted Work as a result of the widespread dissemination of the Copyrighted Work in the United States and Defendant Dr. Gay's studies within the political science arena. Additionally, due to the national acclaim and recognition of the infringed-upon Work, it is highly unlikely that a scholar in the same field would not be knowledgeable of the Work. Specifically, in that the Copyrighted Work had just previously earned one of the highest awards given to a book on government, politics, or international affairs, the Woodrow Wilson Award, as well as other awards and widespread acclaim.

35. Dr. Claudine Gay's work directly infringes on the concept and argument that is laid out in *Black Faces, Black Interests* using much of the same language – without proper attribution to the Work of Dr. Swain – and simply makes the contrary argument. Specifically, Dr. Claudine Gay uses Dr. Carol Swain's original application of the theory of Descriptive Representation verses Substantive Representation to black congressional representation without any attribution or permission. In fact, much if not all, of Dr. Claudine Gay's work uses the same theses as laid out in Dr. Carol Swain's Copyrighted Work and uses the protected Works and Intellectual Property as though it is her original concept or idea, by failing to give proper attribution or gain permission for the use of the protected Work.

36. The first chapter of the Copyrighted Work, titled "The Representation of Black Interests in Congress," contains the heart of the original expression contained within te Copyrighted Work, and Defendant Dr. Gay's *Taking Charge* contains substantial similarities to the Copyrighted Work. Defendant Dr. Gay attempts to present the original expressions of Dr. Swain as her own original thoughts and expressions without the proper accreditation or permission of Dr. Swain. The copying within the Infringing Works contains the cornerstone

Appendix C: My Legal Complaint

and heart of the Copyrighted Work, and Dr. Gay attempts to present the Infringing Works as her own original expressions.

37. In the Infringing Work, *Taking Charge*, Defendant Dr. Gay makes numerous acts of verbatim plagiarism of the Copyrighted Work without properly accrediting the Copyrighted Work, including but not limited to, Dr. Swain's original expression of the meaning of "descriptive" and "substantive representation" as it relates to African Americans in Congress.

38. Dr. Swain uses Hanna Pitkin's definition for descriptive representation as "the statistical correspondence of the demographic characteristics of representatives with those constituents." *Black Faces*, p. 5. Dr. Gay's copying of Dr. Swain's use of the definition fails to cite Swain or Pitkin. Gay uses the identical language without attribution, describing descriptive representation as "the statistical correspondence of the demographic characteristics." *Taking Charge*, p. 2. Dr. Gay takes these original and protected statements and uses them as though they were her original thoughts and ideas as they relate to black congressional representation.

39. Dr. Swain defines substantive representation as "the correspondence between representatives' goals and those of their constituents." *Black Faces*, p. 5. Dr. Gay's copying of Dr. Swain's original expression can be seen by her definition of substantive representation as "the correspondence of legislative goals and priorities." *Taking Charge*, p. 2. Dr. Gay takes these protected statements and uses them as though they were her original thoughts and ideas as they relate to black congressional representation. She cites neither Swain nor Pitkin.

40. Defendant Dr. Gay copied the Copyrighted Work without Plaintiff's authorization, consent, or knowledge, and without any remuneration to Plaintiff.

41. As can be seen from viewing and comparing Exhibits 1 and 4, the Infringing Work, Dr. Gay's dissertation is nearly identical/substantially similar to the thesis of the Copyrighted Work, contained in

chapter one. Like the Copyrighted Work, the Infringing Work utilizes Dr. Swain's original expressions as the central cornerstone of Dr. Gay's dissertation. Given these similarities, the Infringing Product is substantially similar to Plaintiff's Copyrighted Work.

42. The Defendants in this cause of action are extremely versed and experienced parties in the arena of academia. The Harvard Corporation is arguably one of the finest academic institutions, if not the finest. Dr. Claudine Gay was at one time the President of Harvard University, possessing a doctorate and is a Professor of Government and of African and African-American Studies. Additionally, the Defendants have at their disposal numerous individuals and resources that were implemented to review all published works to ensure that infringement does not occur.

43. Since Defendant Dr. Gay copied the Copyrighted Work to create the Infringing Work, she has utilized the Infringing Works to benefit her career success, including but not limited to, rising to the level of President at one of the most prestigious universities in the United Sates. On information and belief, Defendant Harvard continues to publish, sell, and make available for download the Infringing Work on its website, allowing the further dissemination of the Infringing Work. The Defendants are significantly benefitting from the exploitation of Dr. Swain's Copyrighted Works through the publication of the Copyrighted Work; for years Dr. Claudine Gay has risen in the ranks of academia based on the use of the Copyrighted Works and the impression given to others that her dissertation and other works were her original ideas and concepts.

44. Dr. Claudine Gay profited greatly from the use of Dr. Carol Swain's copyrighted work. Gay's dissertation won the Toppan Prize for best political science dissertation in 1998. The Plaintiff contends that her Work was central to Gay's dissertation and the early articles that helped define her career.

45. As a result of her prize-winning dissertation, Dr. Claudine Gay went on to achieve great acclaim in the academic circles, rising to the level of President of Harvard University and earning a salary of

nearly one million dollars ($1,000,000.00) per year. Dr. Gay has benefitted enormously financially and professionally as a result of the improper and infringing use of Dr. Carol Swain's protected Work as though the use were her own original ideas.

46. Dr. Swain was unaware of the plagiarism until December 10, 2023. Dr. Swain contends that Dr. Gay's direct plagiarism and pattern of not adequately citing her work in derivative publications deprived Dr. Swain of citations critically important for career advancement and that it had a ripple effect on her career advancement.

47. The Harvard Corporation has benefitted enormously in the wrongful publication of the Infringing Work as it stands to gain additional acclaim, standing, and publicity over the position it holds in the academic community, through the support of Dr. Claudine Gay's infringement of Dr. Carol Swain's protected Work. The Harvard Corporation has used and benefitted from the Works that Dr. Carol Swain possesses the intellectual property rights to.

48. Dr. Carol Swain never authorized or approved any of the uses of the protected Works for either Defendant.

49. On February 19, 2024, Plaintiff's counsel sent a cease and desist letter to the Defendants objecting to Defendant's unauthorized distribution of the Infringing Work, which was wholly dismissed by the Defendants.

50. To date, the Infringing Works continue to be available to the public, without the proper accreditation of Dr. Swain, and Plaintiff has no evidence that Defendant has complied with the demands set out in Plaintiff's counsel's cease and desist letter.

51. As a result of Defendant's actions described above, Plaintiff has been directly damaged, and is continuing to be damaged, by the unauthorized distribution and sale of the Infringing Works. Defendant has never accounted to or otherwise paid Plaintiff for its use of the Copyrighted Work.

52. Defendant's acts are causing, and unless restrained, will continue

to cause damage and immediate irreparable harm to Plaintiff for which Plaintiff has no adequate remedy at law.

COUNT ONE
Federal Copyright Infringement (17 U.S.C. § 501)

53. Plaintiff repeats and realleges paragraphs 1 through 31 hereof, as if fully set forth herein.

54. The Copyrighted Work is an original literary work containing copyrightable subject matter for which copyright protection exists under the Copyright Act, 17 U.S.C. § 101, et. seq. Plaintiff is the exclusive owner of rights under copyright in and to the Copyrighted Work. Plaintiff owns a valid copyright registration for the Copyrighted Work, attached as Exhibit 2 (not attached here).

55. Through Defendant's conduct alleged herein, including Defendant's reproduction, distribution, and sale of the Infringing Work, which is copied from and substantially similar to Plaintiff's Copyrighted Work, without Plaintiff's permission, Defendant has directly infringed Plaintiff's exclusive rights in the Copyrighted Work in violation of Section 501 of the Copyright Act, 17 U.S.C. § 501.

56. On information and belief, Defendant's infringing conduct alleged herein was and continues to be willful and with full knowledge of Plaintiff's rights in the Copyrighted Work and has enabled Defendants illegally to obtain profit therefrom.

57. As a direct and proximate result of Defendant's infringing conduct alleged herein, Plaintiff has been harmed and is entitled to damages in an amount to be proven at trial. Pursuant to 17 U.S.C. § 504(b), Plaintiff is also entitled to recovery of Defendant's profits attributable to Defendant's infringing conduct alleged herein, including from any and all sales of the Infringing Work and products incorporating or embodying the Infringing Work, and an accounting of and a constructive trust with respect to such profits.

58. Alternatively, Plaintiff is entitled to the maximum statutory damages pursuant to 17 U.S.C. § 504(c), in the amount of $30,000 and

up to $150,000 for Defendant's infringing conduct/for each of Plaintiff's works that Defendant has infringed, and for such other amount as may be proper pursuant to 17 U.S.C. § 504(c).

59. Plaintiff further is entitled to its attorneys' fees and costs pursuant to 17 U.S.C. § 505.

60. As a direct and proximate result of the Defendant's infringing conduct alleged herein, Plaintiff has sustained and will continue to sustain substantial, immediate, and irreparable injury, for which there is no adequate remedy at law. On information and belief, unless Defendant's infringing conduct is enjoined by this Court, Defendant will continue to infringe the Copyrighted Work. Plaintiff therefore is entitled to preliminary and permanent injunctive relief restraining and enjoining Defendant's ongoing infringing conduct.

WHEREFORE, Plaintiff requests judgment against Defendant as follows:

1. That Defendant has violated Section 501 of the Copyright Act (17 U.S.C. § 501).

2. Granting an injunction temporarily and permanently enjoining the Defendants, its employees, agents, officers, directors, attorneys, successors, affiliates, subsidiaries, and assigns, and all of those in active concert and participation with any of the foregoing persons and entities who receive actual notice of the Court's order by personal service or otherwise, from:

(a) manufacturing, distributing, marketing, advertising, promoting, or selling or authorizing any third party to manufacture, distribute, market, advertise, promote, or sell the Infringing Works and any products, works, or other materials that include, copy, are derived from, or otherwise embody the Copyrighted Work;

(b) engaging in any activity that infringes Plaintiff's rights in its Copyrighted Work; and

(c) aiding, assisting, or abetting any other individual or entity in doing any act prohibited by sub-paragraphs (a) or (b).

3. That Defendants be ordered to provide an accounting of Defendant's profits attributable to Defendant's infringing conduct, including Defendant's profits from sales of the Infringing Work and any products, works, or other materials that include, copy, are derived from, or otherwise embody the Copyrighted Work.

4. That Defendant be ordered to destroy or deliver up for destruction all materials in Defendant's possession, custody, or control used by Defendant in connection with Defendant's infringing conduct, including without limitation all remaining copies/inventory of the Infringing Works and any products and works that embody any reproduction or other copy or colorable imitation of the Copyrighted Work, as well as all means for manufacturing them.

5. That Defendant, at its own expense, be ordered to recall the Infringing Works from any distributors, retailers, vendors, or others that have distributed the Infringing Works on Defendant's behalf, and any products, works, or other materials that include, copy, are derived from, or otherwise embody the Infringing Work or the Copyrighted Work, and that Defendant be ordered to destroy or deliver up for destruction all materials returned to it.

6. Awarding Plaintiff:

(d) Defendant's profits obtained as a result of Defendant's infringing conduct, including but not limited to, all profits from sales and other exploitation of the Infringing Work and any products, works, or other materials that include, copy, are derived from, or otherwise embody the Infringing Work or the Copyrighted Work, or in the Court's discretion, such amount as the Court finds to be just and proper;

(e) damages sustained by Plaintiff as a result of Defendant's infringing conduct, in an amount to be proven at trial;

(f) should Plaintiff so elect, statutory damages pursuant to 17 U.S.C. § 504(c) instead of actual damages or profits; and

Appendix C: My Legal Complaint

    (g)   Plaintiff's reasonable attorneys' fees and costs pursuant to 17 U.S.C. § 505.

7. Awarding Plaintiff interest, including pre-judgment and post-judgment interest, on the foregoing sums.

8. Awarding such other and further relief as the Court deems just and proper.

Dated: [DATE]   Respectfully submitted,

    Attorneys for Plaintiff

Appendix D
Excerpts from Claudine Gay's Dissertation Abstract and Introduction: My Comments

Below are excerpts from Claudine Gay's dissertation Abstract as well as pages 1 and 2 of her Introduction, with my commentary sprinkled in between. In doing this, I offer further comparisons and insights about how her dissertation borrows or even outright plagiarizes my key ideas, conclusions and some verbatim verbiage from my book *Black Faces, Black Interests*. Keep in mind that *Black Faces* is an expansion of my extensively researched and properly sourced 1989 PhD dissertation at University of North Carolina at Chapel Hill. After completing my dissertation, I spent an additional two years gathering data and converting the manuscript into the Harvard University Press book that it became. *Black Faces* was originally published in 1993 and expanded in 1995. This was four years before Gay completed her 1997 Harvard PhD dissertation. Her 2001 and 2002 articles on black congressional representation show an awareness of my work. It is listed in the bibliographies of some of the publications. However, it is not discussed in the literature reviews setting up the studies as is traditionally done by scholars.

Gay's dissertation topic was about black congressional representation. From 1995-1998, when Gay was a graduate student at Harvard, *Black Faces, Black Interests* was already a known work in political science and law. It had won three national prizes and had become part of the national dialogue on black congressional representation. It later received three Supreme Court citations in Voting Rights cases. Justice Anthony Kennedy cited *Black Faces*, in *Johnson v. Degrandy*, 512 U.S. 997, 1027 (1994) and Justice Sandra Day O' Connor cited it twice in *Georgia v. Ashcroft*, 539 U.S. (2003). Gay was clearly aware of *Black Faces* because she lists the book in her bibliography, and she used *Black Faces* and an article of mine for select sentences and phrases.

APPENDIX D: CLAUDINE GAY'S DISSERTATION ABSTRACT & INTRO

Evidence from Gay's Abstract:

What was Gay's dissertation about? In her abstract, she states: "Looking past the policy activism of legislators, this book examines instead the impact of black congressional representation on the political behavior and political attitudes of constituents."

Here it puzzled me why she repeatedly referred to her dissertation as "a book." It most certainly was not a book. In fact, she does not have a published book, at least not one I could find at the time I wrote this.

Gay's abstract continues with this description of what the dissertation addresses: "...the impact of black congressional representation on the political behavior and political attitudes of constituents."

Describing her research methodology, Gay writes, "Using both aggregate and survey data, I demonstrate that the presence of black congressional representatives has reshaped the contours of mass politics." . . . [She continues] "Black congressmen have altered the substance of politics by changing the face of the participant community. . . The behavioral response of constituents to black congressional representation is, in part, a function of black electoral styles." . . . [For example] "Black congressmen who eschew provocative rhetoric, and embrace coalitionbuilding, can stem the tide of white political defection. Furthermore, such broad appeals do not compromise their ability to inspire black political engagement."

Clearing my throat, here. The reader should note that *Black Faces, Black Interests* offered case studies of black and white representatives of majority white, black, and mixed legislative districts, as well as roll call data on the voting records of Democrat and Republican members of Congress. Specific to Gay's findings, one of my chapters focused on black representatives of majority-white congressional districts and offered commentary on the representational styles most effective for winning over white voters. In my conclusion, I argued that white voters would support qualified black candidates, and when black candidates lost their election it was often because of their liberal ideologies. The losing black candidates were far more liberal than the white voters they sought to represent.

Evidence from Gay's Introduction (pp. 1-2):

Gay states: "This book weighs the political significance of black electoral success, focusing on the most prominent class of black officeholders: black members of Congress. How has the fact of black congressional representation changed American politics? . . . How has black congressional representation altered the political lives of constituents: what they see in politics and how they behave politically?"

To establish the importance of her dissertation, Gay most apparently used *Black Faces* to set up a strawman. Progressives were really ticked off by my contention that white representatives could represent black constituents and that they sometimes did a better job than their elected black representatives. Drumroll, here! Gay's introduction postulates: "The existence of white officeholders equally likely to support black policy interests would render black office-holding insignificant. Whether there are, in fact, qualitative differences in the agendas and priorities of black office-holders—with favorable implications for how effectively they serve the interests of black constituents—remains a point of contention. However, that policy consequences are the appropriate subject of inquiry has not been a matter of debate."

Okay! There you have it.

Gay's dissertation would not have existed in its present form without the pilfering of ideas and concepts from *Black Faces, Black Interests*. There would have been no problem with her challenging and expanding the ideas, but to ignore the work and pretend that it did not shape her ideas and thinking, is—and was—a clear violation of academic integrity and Harvard's own standards about plagiarism.

I rest my case!

Author Bio

BORN INTO ABJECT POVERTY IN RURAL SOUTHWEST VIRGINIA, Dr. Carol Swain, a high school dropout, went on to earn five degrees. Holding a PhD from the University of North Carolina at Chapel Hill and an MSL from Yale, she also earned early tenure at Princeton and full professorship at Vanderbilt where she was professor of political science and a professor of law. Today she is a sought-after cable news contributor, a best-selling author, a prominent national speaker, and an entrepreneur.

In addition to having three Presidential appointments, Dr. Swain is a former Distinguished Senior Fellow for Constitutional Studies with the Texas Public Policy Foundation who has also served on the Tennessee Advisory Committee to the U.S. Civil Rights Commission, the National Endowment for the Humanities, and the 1776 Commission. Currently, she is a senior fellow with the Institute for Faith and Culture.

An award-winning political scientist, cited three times by the U.S. Supreme Court, she has now authored or edited 13 published books, including the bestseller *Black Eye for America: How Critical Race Theory is Burning Down the House*. Among the others are *Countercultural Living: What Jesus Has to Say About Life, Marriage, Race, Gender, and Materialism*; and *The Adversity of Diversity: How the Supreme Court's Decision to Remove Race from College Admissions Criteria will Doom Diversity Programs*.

Author Bio

Dr. Swain is an expert on civil rights laws, critical race theory, American politics, evangelicalism, and race relations. Her television appearances include BBC Radio and TV, CSPAN, *ABC's Headline News*, CBS, CNN, Fox News, Newsmax, and more.

In addition, she has published opinion pieces in the *New York Times*, the *Washington Post*, the *Wall Street Journal*, the *Epoch Times*, the *Financial Times,* and *USA Today.*

She is the founder and CEO of Carol Swain Enterprises, REAL Unity Training Solutions, Your Life Story for Descendants, and her nonprofit, Be the People.

Dr. Swain is a mother, grandmother, and great-grandmother. She resides in Nashville, Tennessee.

www.ingramcontent.com/pod-product-compliance
Lightning Source LLC
Chambersburg PA
CBHW031701310325
24362CB00008B/165